Amazing Fishing Stories

Amazing Fishing Stories

Paul Knight

WILEY NAUTICAL

Library of Congress Cataloging-in-Publication Data

ISBN: 978-1-119-97033-0

A catalogue record for this book is available from the British Library.

WILEY ⊛ NAUTICAL

Wiley Nautical—sharing your passion.

At Wiley Nautical we're passionate about anything that happens in, on or around the water.

Wiley Nautical used to be called Fernhurst Books and was founded by a national and European sailing
champion. Our authors are the leading names in their fields with Olympic gold medals around their
necks and thousands of sea miles in their wake. Wiley Nautical is still run by people with a love of
sailing, motorboating, surfing, diving, kitesurfing, canal boating and all things aquatic.

Visit us online at www.wileynautical.com for offers, videos, podcasts and more.

Set in 12/14pt Garamond by Aptara Inc., New Delhi, India
Printed in Great Britain by TJ International Ltd, Padstow, Cornwall

To Angela and Archie

CONTENTS

CONTENTS

CONTENTS

ACKNOWLEDGEMENTS

Undertaking the research for this book has been great fun, ranging from talks in tackle shops to after-dinner reminiscences and the occasional hilarious, not to say extraordinary, lunch. On one occasion, I sat down to a meal with Steve Edge, Robert Sloss and the indefatigable Icelandic salmon conservationist Orri Vigfusson, in the oldest restaurant in London, to discuss serious fisheries politics. Somehow the conversation turned to polar bears, and Orri suddenly delved into his jacket pocket and pulled out a packet of genuine ice bear hair. He had been given it, quite legally, while on recent salmon business in Greenland and was going to use it to tie flies. I don't think the waiter could quite believe what he was witnessing, but to us it was just another of those marvellously surreal incidents that happen around fishermen.

Many people have helped me create this book, the most important of which have been the storytellers:

Bertie Alexander, Hughie Campbell Adamson, Rick Cotterell, Tom Davis, Colin Dredge, Steve Edge, Mark Everard, Robin Gould, Andrew Graham-Stewart, Peter Hayes, John Hotchkiss, Gwilym Hughes, Ben Juckes, Barbara Kershaw, Veronica Kruger, Michael Mann, Martin Salter, Robert Shaw, John Slader, Robert Sloss, Michael Smith, Barry Smithard, Peter Spillett and George Westropp.

ACKNOWLEDGEMENTS

Without their input the project would not have been possible and I am extremely grateful to them all, both for the stories themselves – some of them told to me many years ago by people who, sadly, are no longer here to see them in print – and the huge enjoyment I had from listening to them and then writing them down.

There have been others behind the scenes that have helped enormously too. The commission only came to me through my long friendship with the Hodges family. Quite apart from Peter and Jackie's encouragement to keep writing over the years, Toby very kindly introduced me to Wiley Nautical's Commissioning Editor, Miles Kendall, who was looking for someone to write a manuscript like this. Miles has been a great support during the whole publishing process, not least in laying down a flexible brief that, within his guidelines, allowed me to produce the book that I wanted, and I am very grateful to him and the whole Wiley team.

Some of the storytellers have kindly commented on the drafts of their particular tales, and Veronica Kruger has, as always, added constructive critique. My family has been very supportive too, Angela putting up with countless hours of me sitting on the sofa with the laptop on my knees, while Archie was an enthusiastic reader of every word, demanding to know when the next chapter would be complete long before it was.

To all I give my heartfelt thanks, and hope that the finished book does justice to their support.

INTRODUCTION

Ever since the whale swallowed Jonah, there have been stories about massive fish and the people who hunt them. And just as the whale ultimately lost Jonah, so the tales of those that got away evoke delicious mystery, and give rise to fishing legends.

No one captured this more deeply than Ernest Hemingway in the *The Old Man and the Sea*. Anyone who has ever set out to catch a monster can empathise with the old fisherman, Santiago, in his tiny boat. He hooked and fought a gigantic marlin for days, finally defeating the fish but having to leave it in the water, lashed to the gunwale, because it was too big to come aboard the skiff. Victory turned into despair as one shark after another took bites out of the fish, so that only a skeleton remained by the time Santiago reached port. All the local fishermen could do was to measure what was left, 18 feet of head, bones and tail, while the old man slept away his exhaustion in his house.

We only have memories of the fish we lose, so fact easily turns to myth. I was just 8 years old when I was fishing one day on Brighton's Palace Pier, down on the landing stage among the girders. I had an ancient cane rod of my father's and I was float fishing, I remember, with a hook dangling a few yards beneath the surface, on which was impaled a large chunk of herring. I think I must have seen some mullet cruising around and, not realising that they sipped seaweed and maggots but seldom herring, thought I might catch one like this.

I didn't see the float go under, because I wasn't looking. I just have this vivid recollection of a truly violent pull on the rod, the like of which I had never felt before and seldom since. I didn't see the fish, didn't even hook it, which was just as well, because I think the rod would have immediately collapsed in sympathy. I was left with a feeling of profound shock, which rolls down the years to me still. I stood stunned, wondering what the hell this fishing lark was all about. My father, a clergyman, believed me when I stammered out the tale, but only because, he told me years later, I was sheet white and shaking, and he realised from his experiences as an army chaplain during the war that I was in deep shock over something. I think now that my fish was probably a bass, and I would be well into my teens before I eventually caught one that would, in my mind at least, come even remotely close to my lost leviathan. But that is the beauty of the myth; my mystery fish could, indeed, have been a record catch, and no one can ever prove otherwise.

The attraction is not all about lost monsters, of course. My first fish, the smallest of whiting off Lowestoft Pier, is a treasured memory, although what I remember most of that event was my mother complaining that the fish should really have been returned to *its* mother, not given a premature rap over the head, however proud I was of myself. My first trout, caught in the brook near my home, was a defining moment in my life, although that, too, was difficult to locate in the frying pan. My first salmon – ah, now, that was something else: a pull almost as savage as my mythical bass, and played as though my life depended on landing it. The pleasure of catching that fish was only surpassed when I watched my 11-year-old son take his first salmon from the Lower Tweed. He played his fish much better than his father had done all those years before him, and the closest he came to losing it was when I panicked and tried to grab it far too early.

So, some of the stories in this book are my own, but most have been gleaned from others. They range right across the world, from the UK to Australia and New Zealand, taking in Russia, Alaska, the wild waters of the North West Atlantic, the Caribbean, Florida Keys, and the Indian Ocean, and they touch on the mysteries of India, the

INTRODUCTION

Himalayas and Africa. There are brown trout, Atlantic and Pacific salmon, sea trout, eels, pike, mahseer, tiger fish, black marlin, tuna, bonefish, permit, tarpon and many other species. Some are tales of extraordinary events happening to ordinary people seeking nothing more than a few hours of solitude with a fishing rod. Others involve great characters and big personalities, to whom standout happenings are probably commonplace. They all embrace one central facet, though: a love of fish and fishing, and the truly wonderful places across the globe to which the species and the sport draw us, and the people we meet when we get there. And then, of course, there is the wildlife, often extremely mischievous, which adds terrific spice to some of these tales.

I hope you enjoy this anthology. All the stories are based on actual events, although I trust you will forgive my own embellishments here and there. There are a few ghost stories as well, and some of you will, I am sure, scoff that these couldn't possibly be based on fact. All I can say is that the people concerned obviously thought that their experiences were real enough, and I'm certainly not going to suggest otherwise.

So most of what you read in these pages is based on the truth. Although you never quite know with fisherman, but that just makes listening to their stories all the more fun. . .

PART ONE

Captured Monsters

SALMON ON THE FLOOD

The North Esk can be a dangerous place for a wading angler, because heavy rain can raise water levels alarmingly quickly. That is exactly what happened during an extraordinary fight that required courage, friendship and no little luck.

The North Esk is one of Scotland's more prolific salmon and sea trout rivers. The proprietor of this middle-beat fishery, Hughie, and a friend, Simon, were on the river early one morning, having seen a weather forecast the previous evening that promised rain by midday. The river was already at a good height for fly fishing, but it wouldn't need much of a deluge to make it unfishable, which would be a pity, because there were plenty of fresh salmon about.

It was September and some stale sea trout were being a nuisance. Both men had caught and returned a couple of fish in the lower pools, but Hughie was now back at the top of the beat in the Junction Pool, a classic taking spot at this river height. It had started to drizzle and some weeds, leaves and twigs were now floating past, a sure sign that it was already raining in the hills and the river was beginning to rise. Time was running out but the water still felt 'right', as far as Hughie was concerned, so he kept rolling out a stoat's tail and mending the line so that it fished as slowly as possible across the rising flow.

He was halfway down the pool when Simon appeared.

'Any luck?' asked Hughie.

'Another dark sea trout, but no salmon. I've seen plenty, but they just won't take.'

'The fish are getting twitchy with this rise in water; they're head and tailing all over the place up here, so I reckon one's got to take in a minute. Fish down behind me.'

No sooner had he said it than Hughie had a good draw on the line as the fly reached mid-channel. He lifted the rod and was into a fish, at which point, about 15 yards below, a very stale sea trout of 4 or 5 pounds leapt clear of the water.

'Another kipper,' said Simon and turned to walk to the head of the pool.

The head shaking and solid weight on the line didn't feel like a sea trout. 'That wasn't my fish!' Hughie called out. 'Honestly, Simon, this feels a bit more serious!'

Simon came back as the line started to leave the reel at a steady speed against a tightened brake and a full bend in the 15-foot rod. Just then, at the bottom of the pool, where it runs into a glide, a tail appeared out of the water.

'Bloody hell, Hughie!'

'Told you! That's the biggest tail I've seen in this river for years!'

He managed to stop the fish on that first run and recover some line, but then it was off downstream again, far more energetically this time, as though it had just woken up to the fact that something was wrong. It ran into the shallower water below, which was quickly being turned into a foaming rapid by the rising river.

'You'll have to follow it,' said Simon. 'You've got no chance of bringing it back against that volume of water.'

'Okay, but stay with me; this looks hairy.'

Hughie followed the fish, trying to keep some sort of contact and only giving line when he had to. He didn't want too much fly line on the water: it would create impossible drag in those conditions and could easily pull the hook free from what he was now convinced was the fish of the season. He was getting soaking wet from shipping water over his chest waders, plus the drizzle that had now evolved into a monsoon, but he was oblivious to that for the moment as he concentrated completely on his line cutting through the water.

The fish bore remorselessly downstream and all he could do was follow; the maximum side strain he dared use wasn't making the slightest impression on its progress. They went through the rapids and into the next pool, where the fish at least slowed a little in the deeper water, giving Hughie and Simon a chance to catch up. They were still wading, because there was too much vegetation on the bank to play it safely from up there.

'Er, Hughie, I reckon that water's up by a foot since I was here half an hour ago. This is getting crazy.'

'Look, get back to dry land. I'll give it some stick for five minutes and see if I can bully it out. I'm not letting this go without one more effort.'

'I'm staying here: you need someone with a bit of sense around this situation.'

The fight went on much longer than five minutes. The rain kept pouring down and Hughie could see the river rising in front of his eyes. The flow was appreciably stronger now, and not only was the water perilously close to the top of his chest waders, he was finding it increasingly difficult to stay upright. Fish of the season or not, the situation was getting stupid.

'Come on, Hughie, just give the bloody thing some welly! You've only got two chances anyway, and we'll die if we stay out here much longer.'

Hughie lent back and bent the rod as far as it would go, and the salmon started to come. For the first time, he felt he had some sort of control over the fish, and he looked behind him to see where on the bank he could land it. The water was now so high that there was hardly any bank left. If he did this right, he could practically float the salmon onto dry land.

Then it all went wrong again. The fish suddenly woke up, turned around and shot straight out of the second pool into the one below. The two pools were separated by a stone croy, on which was growing a substantial sycamore bush, which in normal water wasn't a problem. As though the salmon knew all this, it turned left and took the line behind the croy.

'That's enough,' Hughie called out. 'I can't get past the tree and the river's getting too dangerous. Time to break off and get the hell out of here!'

'No way!' Simon took the huge salmon net off his back and drove himself through the water towards the croy. 'I've had a change of heart. It's got personal now and I'm not letting this bugger get the better of us. Just hold him there if you can.'

'Careful! It's a bloody sight deeper on the other side of the. . .'

His warning came too late. Simon had already clambered over the croy and was now actually swimming. He disappeared behind the bush and Hughie was operating completely blind, hands above his head and clamped on the reel so that the salmon was kept at least somewhere close to Simon.

'Can you reach it?'

'I can see it! Four more yards my way and I can get it!'

Hughie wound down the rod tip, the line now seemingly running through the middle of the bush, then hauled back and shipped two boots full of water over the back of his waders. His arm muscles were screaming and he had no idea what was happening the other end. Then the fish started bouncing the rod around and he had to start playing it all over again.

'For god's sake, Hughie, give me some line! Slacken off completely!'

Bewildered by the command, Hughie let the line go and waited for further instruction from his invisible friend. Then, from behind the bush, Simon appeared, seemingly treading water in his waders and pulling a bulging net along with him.

'You flaming hero!' Hughie cried, and waded over to haul a bedraggled and half-drowned Simon back across the croy. Between them, they dragged the net over to the bank, somehow managed to crawl out and then collapsed onto soggy wet land, coughing up water and completely exhausted.

'Look at the *size* of it!' Simon cried.

'Bloody hell, it must go 30 pounds. And look, the hook's fallen out. That's lucky.'

Simon slapped him on the shoulder. 'You don't know the half of it!'

It transpired that Simon had been hanging onto the bush with one hand while making a desperate netting lunge with the other. The fish had moved its head at the wrong moment and the net had actually knocked the fly out of its jaws, whereupon the treble hook had become caught in the net as the freed fish disappeared from sight. So, for a good half minute, Hughie had been playing the net in Simon's hands, not the fish.

'I was trying to decide how the hell I was going to tell you I'd lost your fish,' Simon explained. 'Then this dark shape appeared below me, and gradually rose up and became more and more silvery. That's when I screamed at you to give me line so that I could free the net and scoop the ruddy fish into it! It was obviously just as knackered by the fight as you look right now.'

The fish weighed 32 pounds, Hughie's biggest ever salmon. The story did the rounds, of course, and a couple of weeks later the Chairman of the Esk Fishery Board called him.

After hearing about the fight at first hand, he laughed down the phone. 'I'm not sure that fish was strictly legal. I've been looking through the old records, and your family gave up its salmon-netting rights in 1872. . .'

WORLD RECORD IN
A ROWING BOAT

Catching huge sea fish from big motorboats, with powerful engines to help with the fight, is one thing, but how about taking on a marine leviathan from an open skiff with nothing more than a set of oars for propulsion?

In the early years of sea fishing, with only primitive tackle available, no one seriously considered trying to catch a blue-fin tuna on rod and line. That was until 1911, when a Canadian millionaire racehorse breeder, JKL Ross, first realised that blue fins migrated to the waters off Cape Breton Island, Nova Scotia, every year. He was managing director of his father's British Empire Steel Company at the time, and often took his boat over to St Ann's Bay for Sunday lunches. It was here that he saw blue fins beating up bait shoals on the surface and, being a sportsman, decided he would try to catch one. He succeeded on 28 August by landing a fish of 680 pounds, the world's first blue fin caught on rod and line and, hence, the inaugural world record for the species. And just to add some spice to the capture, he didn't fish from a powered boat, but from an 18-foot double-ended rowing skiff!

The idea of catching tuna from small boats not only caught other fishermen's imagination, it became the accepted way of tackling blue fins, especially during the heyday of the North East English coast fishery, which was based at Scarborough. Back in Nova Scotia, many big specimens were landed on Cape Breton Island and the record was regularly bettered, although the runs of tuna were beginning to dwindle by 1950. One of the most avid fishermen at this time was Jack Ross's son-in-law, Duncan Hodgson.

Duncan, a Commander in the Canadian Navy, was a hunter with an experimental streak. He loved fishing for tuna, especially in the same challenging way as Jack had done. So, with his retained boatman, Percy MacRitchie, who had also been on the oars for Jack Ross's 1911 fish, he set about building a similar double-ended 18-footer. The only luxury he afforded himself was a shallow hole in the midsection seat where he could anchor the rod butt. The rest would be a straight fight between him and the blue fins: man to fish, so to speak, with more than a passing nod to Ernest Hemingway.

The technique was simple. A motor tender would tow them out into St Ann's Bay, an area about 4 miles long by a mile wide, and then Percy would take over on the oars once they sighted tuna. The tuna herded baitfish into the bay, gorging themselves on the shoals of herring, mackerel and squid, and the idea was to try to head them off with the boat, often trolling the bait right through the middle of a feeding frenzy, and hope that a tuna would hook up.

Duncan began to catch plenty of blue fins this way, and locals watching from boats or the shore would tell of the most incredible spectacles, with the rowing boat being towed like an express train across the Bay, faster than the motor-boat tenders could keep up, Duncan hanging onto the rod while Percy tried desperately to control the boat and stop it from capsizing. The fights would often last for hours before Percy could use the gaff. Once the fish was taken ashore and weighed, Duncan would celebrate the capture with as much alcoholic alacrity as his physical endeavour during the battle.

During the 1950 season, Duncan and Percy had seen a few small shoals of tuna containing fish in the 400–500-pound bracket. However, they had also periodically spotted the odd larger fish, which tended to remain solitary hunters. One of these was very large indeed, quite the biggest fish they had ever seen, and Duncan set his heart on catching the monster before the season was out.

Day after day they trolled St Ann's Bay in the hope that the tuna would grab the bunch of mackerel impaled on the huge hook, but they only caught the occasional standard-sized 'school' fish, as Duncan referred to anything under 500 pounds. Then, on 4 September, with Percy looking weary on the oars and not a sniff of a fish all afternoon, Duncan hailed the tender, *Sea Pigeon,* to tow them back to harbour. As Percy eased off the rowing, the boat lost its way and the mackerel bait sank deeper into the bay, although Duncan, standing up now with the rod crooked under his arm, was not conscious of the fact, and was certainly under the impression that his fishing was over for the day. However, as the tender drew near, the rod tip was suddenly pulled violently downwards, and Duncan only just reacted quickly enough to keep hold of the butt.

The tuna bore away deeper, pulling line off the huge multiplier reel. 'Bloody lucky, Percy!' Duncan shouted. 'Feels a good fish, too.'

'Must be a big solitary one,' drawled Percy, 'as we ain't seen any school fish today. Perhaps it's *the* big one.'

After the first run, the fight settled down into dogged attrition, with the tuna trying to stay deep and circling the boat, always to the left, and Duncan hanging on desperately, allowing the fish to tire itself by towing the boat round St Ann's Bay. Whenever the fish stopped and tried to sulk under the boat, Percy would row away and change the line angle, which encouraged the fish to take off on another run and, hopefully, hasten its exhaustion. In this way, Duncan gradually gained the upper hand and he finally brought the tuna to the surface after a relatively short, 80-minute struggle.

Duncan then realised why the fish had been circling more than running straight. The line was lying diagonally across its back and had been pulling against the opposite side of its tail. At this point the line sprung free, and the fish set off on one last, 200-metre dash, coming completely out of the water as it did and showing off its colossal size.

Duncan then managed to turn the fish towards him, and was able to pump it back to the boat. Percy eased them into the shore, then jumped out and gaffed the fish up onto the beach. They roped it through the gills and round the tail, and then called in the *Sea Pigeon* to haul it back into harbour.

In the boathouse, a pair of old scales, weighing up to 1000 pounds, hung from a wooden rafter. Duncan and Percy dragged the fish into the shed, stuck a steel hook into its gills and hauled it up onto the scales. As soon as its tail was clear of the floor, the needle shot round to the 1000-pound marker, there was a loud metallic twang and the ancient spring mechanism collapsed.

'Right, Percy, plan B. Ring for a truck and we'll take it into town.'

Percy made the phone call, then announced that the lorry wouldn't arrive for a couple of hours. Not requiring any further excuse, Duncan produced a bottle of whisky and the celebrations began, as did the discussion about whether this was the fish they had been stalking all season, and if there had ever been a bigger blue fin landed into Cape Breton Island; or, indeed, anywhere else.

As the whisky flowed, so did the banter and the idea of a possible record became more and more of an issue for Duncan. In particular, he became increasingly concerned with the loss of blood from the mighty fish, both from the hole in its flank from Percy's gaff and the wound in the gills where the scales' hook had lodged. The floor was swimming in blood.

'Look, Percy, it isn't fair that we're losing all this weight. We need to compensate.'

'Okay, boss, how?'

'Stones: get some rocks from the beach!'

Duncan lowered the tuna and forced open its cavernous mouth, whereupon Percy stuffed miniature boulders down its gullet. They estimated the weight of rock required to replace the blood loss, then added a few more for good measure.

The truck duly arrived and drove them round to St Ann's Harbour, where they found a reliable set of scales that would provide an authentic weight for the record books. The fish was hauled up by the tail. . . whereupon the rocks promptly fell out from the mouth, to the hilarity of the assembled crowd.

Once Duncan had charmed his way out of the embarrassment, and they were sure no boulders were left in the fish, the weight was officially set at 977 pounds, a new world record for blue-fin tuna by more than 20 pounds. The fish measured 9 feet, 9 inches in length.

Over more celebratory whisky, the discussions went on, especially about the true weight of the fish as it would have been when it first came out of the water.

'Blood loss and six hours' dehydration,' Duncan mused, 'must have taken a few pounds off. How many d'you reckon, Percy?'

'Thirty, boss.'

'Easily that. The records can say what they like, but we caught a 1000-pounder today, Percy, I'm convinced of it.'

As a postscript, Duncan lost another massive tuna, visibly bigger than his record fish, after it towed the boat for 16 miles and he actually had it on the surface ready to gaff. Then, freakishly, the swivel at the top of the trace touched the boat's gunwale and sprang the quick-release locking mechanism, and the fish was gone.

However, his record stood for a further 20 years, when it was beaten by just a few pounds. And then, in 1979, a colossal fish was taken off the coast of Nova Scotia that weighed a smidgeon under 1500 pounds. That would have seemed an impossible dream to Jack Ross back in 1911, but he and Duncan Hodgson would surely be proud that their pioneering legacy lives on. Now the challenge for the future is to ensure that unsustainable commercial pressure on the fantastic blue-fin tuna does not condemn the species merely to distant memories and record books.

ATTRITION AND SLIME

Playing and landing a fish is sometimes only half the battle – especially if it's a big conger eel with a bad attitude.

As Ernest Hemingway's Old Man found out the hard way, playing a big fish is only half the story. Having battled your quarry to the surface, you have to land it, despatch it and then decide what to do with it afterwards, all of which can sometimes prove spectacularly difficult. The Old Man, of course, failed in his bid to transport his giant marlin back to port intact. A couple of decades after *The Old Man and the Sea* was published, during a sea-fishing trip and its aftermath, Barry Smithard had very nearly as exhaustive an all-round battle on his hands as Hemingway's famous character.

Barry was with a group of friends on a boat trip out of Dover. Fishing had only just started in the morning and a few pollock and some small ling had already come aboard. The portents for a reasonable catch were good, although Barry was after bigger quarry, for which he was using tackle that was, to say the least, unconventional. At the end of his line was a large, spoon-type spinner made from half of a pair of old Vincent motorcycle handlebars, to which were attached, via swivels, a wire trace and a large single hook, onto which was speared a side of mackerel as bait. The half handlebar had been hammered flat and then twisted to make it spin in the current. The total length of this somewhat unconventional 'Vincent and mackerel' set-up was 15 inches.

Barry had a tentative bite and initially thought that he had snagged the wreck over which they were fishing. Then the wreck moved, and he realised that something live and rather heavy was on the other end. He leaned into the fish and felt the first head shake transmit itself up the line.

'Conger,' said the skipper confidently.

Barry nodded, trying hard to pump the fish away from the wreck. 'Good one too by the feel of it.'

As is often the case with big conger, it became a dour fight, with Barry winning back line, only to lose it again as the fish bored back towards the wreck. A war of attrition ensued for a good 20 minutes before the eel finally broke surface.

'Blimey!' cried the skipper. 'We ain't had one that big for years!'

The conger kept shaking its head and body like a snake, trying to move backwards across the surface away from the boat. Another few minutes of brute force wrestling went by until Barry eventually brought the conger close enough for the skipper to reach. The gaff was plunged in behind the eel's head and it was hauled, writhing and viciously shaking its head, over the gunwale and onto the deck.

A farcical dance then took place. The conger, still attached to Barry's line, proceeded to chase the anglers round the boat, while the skipper dived into the wheelhouse for the weapon he kept there for just this sort of event. He came out brandishing a lead-weighted baseball bat and joined in the impromptu conga line of wary fishermen and angry eel.

Some order was restored when the skipper managed to grab the wire trace with his gloved hand, but he then made the mistake of placing his left boot too close to the conger's head as he prepared to thump it. Before he could land a decent blow, the conger's teeth latched on to his boot.

'Sod it! Make it let go!' he yelled.

A tug-of-war ensued, with Barry on the gaff and the boatman grimly pulling at his boot. This impasse continued until the conger's vice-like mouth-hold tore the front off the boatman's boot and Barry went flying sternwards, ending up prostrate on the deck with the eel in his lap. It didn't bite him because its teeth were already set on mangling the ripped-off toe-end of the skipper's rubber footwear.

Barry managed to push the eel away and scramble clear. At last, the skipper, toes poking through the hole in his boot, landed a blow on the conger's head with the baseball bat, momentarily stunning the fish. Making good use of his temporary advantage, he grabbed a long-handled bait-cutting blade and cut through the monofilament just above the trace. He then attempted to kick the eel with his one good boot towards the open hatch into the fish hold.

Unfortunately, the kick only succeeded in waking up the conger, which, now completely free from the line, started thrashing around again and snapping at anything vaguely human that came into its line of sight. It took the skipper, Barry and two others another couple of minutes before they were able to master the situation and finally topple the eel over the edge of the hatch into the void below. All four then sat on the deck gasping for breath, thankful that one toeless rubber boot was the only lasting damage inflicted on them or the boat.

'Good fun this sea fishing, isn't it?' Barry suggested.

The skipper nodded. 'Yeah, but keep to bloody pouting and mackerel for the rest of the day, if you wouldn't mind.'

They steamed back to Dover harbour in the late afternoon. Having taken all the tackle and other fishing paraphernalia off the boat onto the quayside, they couldn't stave off the moment any longer.

'D'you think it's dead?' Barry asked warily.

'Bloody well better be, otherwise it can stay where it is till morning,' said the skipper.

Down in the fish room they gingerly prodded the eel, but there was no reaction, and the gleam of battle seemed to have gone from its eyes. Barry very carefully placed a rubbish bag over its head, but it only reached so far down the body. Another bag was drawn up from the tail end, and they eventually managed to encompass the whole eel in black plastic. They hauled it first onto the deck and then onto the quay, where they plonked it on the scales. It went a scintilla over 60 pounds.

'That's the biggest ever from my boat,' said the skipper. 'What are you going to do with it now?'

'Take it home and eat it. My father's rather partial to eel.'

It was after midnight when Barry arrived at his house. His immediate problem was that, after six hours in a fish hold and a similar time in the boot of the car while supper was eaten, a couple of pints drunk and he had driven home, it was probably advisable to take some conservation measures, otherwise the fish might not be edible by morning. He took a large box of sea salt from the kitchen, grabbed the plastic-covered eel in both arms and staggered up the stairs as quietly as he could, mindful that the rest of the household was fast asleep. He eased the eel into the bath, covered it with cold water and added a plentiful dollop of salt to help the preservation process. He then showered off the smell of eel and retired to bed.

In the morning, the conger was still lying in the bath, but Barry now discovered that a fish, especially an eel, becomes very slimy indeed if left in salted water for any length of time. So the challenge was how to get a heavy, wet and exceptionally slippery fish from the bathroom down to the kitchen without covering the newly fitted carpet on the landing, staircase and hall in conger slime.

Barry's instinct told him that he had more chance of success if he abandoned the direct, internal route and went instead for an exterior strategy. He opened the bathroom window and carefully plotted a suitable course, taking into account that the gravitational force on a 60-pound conger eel could very easily create havoc below if everything went pear shaped. He picked up the fish and, with extreme care, slipped it out through the window.

The eel's progress was slowed slightly by sliding it down the roof tiles of the kitchen extension until it reached the sloping roof of the conservatory a few feet below. Here, aided by the lubricating properties of the salt-enhanced slime, it gathered pace so that, on reaching the edge of the roof, it was catapulted into mid-air at a velocity that saw it clear the patio and shoot into the back garden. It finally came to rest in a rigour-held, semi-circular, water-feature-style heap in the middle of the lawn. It lay there, gazing back at the house with lifeless eyes, suggesting that this was no way for a proud conger to end its days.

After breakfast, Barry armed himself with a large kitchen knife and a hacksaw. He proceeded to cut up the eel, still on the lawn, into meal-sized cutlets, which he wrapped up and placed in the freezer. The eel kept the family in fish suppers for the rest of the year and everyone agreed that it was excellent, particularly in fish pie.

'Mind you, we had to be innovative with the recipes,' Barry declared, 'just so we didn't get fed up with eating ruddy conger eel for the umpteenth time. I tend to stick to fly-fishing these days: it isn't too demanding and the eating is good, but perhaps the sense of adventure isn't quite the same!'

BROWNIE OF A LIFETIME

Fishing for brown trout in the rivers of New Zealand is considered by many to be the ultimate test for game anglers. And if you're lucky enough to hook one, especially an outlandishly big one, they fight like no other brown trout on earth.

There tend to be a few large, territorial fish in each New Zealand river location, which can be hard to spot and fiendishly difficult to approach. And, once in position, you have to be deadly accurate with the cast so as not to disturb the famously spooky fish. The slightest error, and they melt away like ghosts.

John Hotchkiss had fished all over the world and produced a successful television series, *The Take*, which featured game-fishing venues from many different countries. This trip to New Zealand was in advance of the crew arriving to film one of the episodes, and was to be on a private river in the Buller District on the west side of the South Island, as a guest of the Western Rivers Lodge. All he knew was that he would be stalking fish with an experienced local guide, and that he should expect quality rather than quantity.

The bumpy 4x4 trip out to the Buller system showed up the stunning variety of the island's landscape, a rich tapestry of rainforest, rivers, lakes and towering, snow-capped mountains and glaciers. It was the most fantastic backdrop to a fishing trip that John could imagine and he was already looking at the place from a producer's eye. Even before he wet a line, he knew this would make a fantastic episode for *The Take*.

At the lodge, he was introduced to his guide, John Gendall, who looked at him and then his tackle.

'Your camouflage clothing's fine, but forget the white fly line; the fish will see it a mile off in this water. You can use one of my green lines.'

He was right: the water was brilliantly clear and flowing translucent green from the snow melt in the mountain streams. But unlike the English chalkstreams, there was no profusion of life, no shoals of fish darting in and out of weed-choked channels. Rather, the river was deep, with a gravel bed and a profusion of boulders that should be providing the perfect habitat for wild brown trout. Except that, initially at least, John couldn't see any fish.

Gendall walked him slowly up the bank, inspecting the water through his Polaroids with the intensity that only a professional guide can produce. He suddenly stopped, then took John's shoulder and pointed at a spot about three-quarters of the way across the river. John searched frantically through the water column and gradually a fish-like shape emerged into his vision, blurred by the movement of 4 feet of water over its back and the fact that it was lying beside a rock, making it look like just another part of the general riverscape. He would have walked straight past it had he been on his own, and yet he usually prided himself on being able to spot fish as well as anyone. This was a completely different dimension to the sort of fishing he was used to.

He put on a weighted pheasant tail and cast above the fish, so as to give the fly time to sink somewhere near the right level. The fly line went a fraction too far, however, and the fish must have seen the shadow, because it disappeared.

'Bad luck,' muttered Gendall.

'Heck, they don't give you much of a chance, do they?'

Gendall grinned. 'Not much, no.'

The afternoon ended without a fish and John feeling rather chastened by the experience. He had cast at four beautiful trout, all over 3 pounds, but not one had been tempted to give the fly even a cursory glance. And they had spooked all too easily.

'Right,' said Gendall over a beer in the lodge, 'that's the introduction bit over. Tomorrow we'll go after some proper fish, but you've got to forget your chalkstream fishing from home; I've done that and it's kid's stuff compared to this. Here you have to spot your fish and think completely *natural*. These are truly wild trout and they don't get to their size by being stupid: they're far cuter than anything you'll find back in the UK. So keep low, eyes open and dead accurate casting in the morning, okay?'

Gendall chose a stretch of river relevant to the wind direction in the morning, the idea being to avoid having to cast into a strong downstream breeze. Still feeling a bit like the new boy at school, John walked beside Gendall up the bank and, just as the day before, was stopped in his tracks by his guide's arm.

'Now, that's a fish, John,' Gendall whispered, and pointed midstream.

It took John a moment to pick out the trout and then his jaw dropped. 'Bloody hell, it must be 5, 6 pounds?'

'Eight, I'd say; he's a good 5 feet down, don't forget.'

Despite the size of the fish and the water depth, John reckoned he might come to the dry, so he tried first a Royal wolf and then a blue blow fly. Not a flicker of interest to the wolf, but the trout did come and look at the blow fly. John's heart missed a couple of beats as it rose through the water, but then it turned away at the last moment and sank back to its lair, where it remained unmoved by further offerings.

'I think you've got more chance with a nymph,' suggested Gendall.

John was using a 4-pound breaking-strain leader because of the clarity of the water. He lengthened this to account for the depth and tied on a small piece of white fluff as a bite indicator, then chose a size 16 pheasant-tail nymph, weighted to get down through the water column quickly. He then waded quietly into the edge of the current and made half a dozen upstream casts. They all landed roughly in the right place, which was something of a result, seeing as the wind had suddenly changed and was now coming into his face. The fish remained unmoved, but at least it hadn't been spooked, so John changed up to a size 14 pheasant tail and made another couple of casts. Still no reaction.

'Okay, I think he's seen it overhead too much,' said Gendall. 'Come this way a bit. Change the fly's angle . . . good, now more left and six inches further upstream . . . yeah, let that come past him.'

John's eyes were glued to the white fluff at the exact moment that it merely stuttered, almost imperceptibly, in its drift. And what he was most proud of was that he reacted instantly and hit the fish a fraction of a second before Gendall shouted for him to do so. Then everything went manic!

'On the bank, John. Quick, give me your hand!'

The trout charged across to the other side of the river, then came back at a similar speed, seemingly in as much panic as John felt himself. He had no idea how many fish he had caught in different parts of the world, but none had ever made his legs shake like they were doing right then. He staggered onto the bank, thankful there was someone 30 years his junior to haul him out, and then it was a case of following the fish downstream, where it was now heading with serious purpose.

'Keep the rod high,' advised Gendall. 'If it wants to run, just. . . *Jeeesus!*'

The fish had jumped clear of the water and John's split-second impression was that it could easily have been a big sea trout from some South American river, so deep and silver was its body. He stifled his panic and remembered Gendall's advice about playing New Zealand trout: 'keep everything smooth; no jerky movements, or you'll lose them for sure'.

Forty hyperactive, exhausting minutes later, and 300 yards downstream from where the trout had taken, John managed to encourage it into the shallows. Gendall then tried to land it, but failed on the first three attempts because it wouldn't stay in the net. His fourth effort succeeded, just, and John was able to drop the rod and fall to his knees in the water beside his fish.

Gendall tapped him on the shoulder. 'Forget 8 pounds, matey, this is the bloody fish of a lifetime. Look at the *girth* on it!'

John was stunned and his brain wouldn't focus. 'That's the best-conditioned brownie I've ever set eyes on,' was all he could think to say. And it was: a magnificent, perfectly proportioned hen fish, silver flanked and with numerous bold black spots.

They took measurements and photographs and returned the fish to the river, where it recovered almost immediately and glided serenely away to lie beside a boulder opposite them, as though nothing untoward had ever happened. Then there was much hand shaking and back slapping, and the grin on Gendall's face said it all: this was as much a triumph for him as it was for John.

They sat and ate their lunch, which was made all the better because they could still see the fish holding station right in front of them. Gendall did the weight calculations by comparing the trout's length and girth measurements against his chart – and sucked in his breath at the result. 'At *least* 16 pounds, probably a shade more. *Unbelievable*, especially on a 4-pound line!'

They were the toast of the Lodge, not to mention the film crew the following week. And the toast continues to this day, because the Western Rivers Lodge has never had a bigger brown trout landed, nor have the guides seen a better fish. And as for John, a cast of the brownie hangs above the fireplace in his Wiltshire home, a constant reminder of his greatest angling feat.

BANANAS, COCA-COLA
AND TARPON

Fizzy drinks and fruit seem a strange recipe for catching one of the world's hardest fighting, most acrobatic fish – but they worked their magic for one fortunate fisherman.

B y the time Colin reached his 50th birthday, he was a well-respected member of Wiltshire's Salisbury fishing society in the UK. Working in a tackle dealer's shop in the city centre, and a well-known angler around Wiltshire and Hampshire coarse and trout fisheries, he reached his half-century as a highly popular, jovial soul who knew as much as most about modern fishing tackle and tactics. He had caught many notable fish, including a rainbow trout a shade under 20 pounds from a local lake. He also did some sea fishing, but he never set foot on a boat. Just looking at one moored up alongside a harbour pontoon was enough to make him feel violently seasick, and so he very definitely stayed put on terra firma.

He was expecting nothing more for his birthday celebrations than a few drinks and a slap-up family meal in a decent Salisbury restaurant. He was still thinking that when two of his friends, Peter and Paul, took him to one side in the shop.

'We've arranged your birthday bash,' they told him. 'Everything's organised.'

'Thanks, guys, which pub are we going to?'

'Er. . . a bar in Florida, probably.'

'*Florida*? The USA?'

'That's right,' said Peter. 'We're going to the Keys, you, me and him. You're joining our annual fishing party.'

'When?'

'Saturday.'

'But. . .'

'Richard's organised the shop rota, and Hannah's made sure your passport's ready and you've got the right clothes to take. We've thought of everything.'

A British Airways Atlantic flight later, they were ensconced in a fabulous Key-side bungalow with the rest of Peter's party, all Americans. There was beer and food in the fridge, and information about the fishing they would be doing in the morning. Only one thing was getting in the way of this being an idyllic 50th-birthday trip for Colin: the fishing was scheduled to be from a boat. And not a very big boat at that.

In the morning, the party members were having breakfast – except, of course, for Colin. He was eyeing up the dory on the mooring at the end of the garden. There wasn't any wind and he knew they weren't going out into the open ocean, but he could feel his stomach already responding to the very thought of being afloat. He was convinced that he would start retching the moment he stepped aboard, and his legs started to wobble merely thinking about it.

Paul had a worried expression on his face. 'Heavens, Colin, you're shaking like a leaf. Don't worry, it's flat calm out there, millpond smooth, honestly.'

'Can't help it,' Colin spluttered. 'I *hate* boats! Can't I fish from the shore?'

'No way,' said Peter. 'You haven't come all this way just to fish from the bank. The captain says the tarpon are out in the middle, so that's where we're going.'

'I don't think. . .'

One of the Americans, 'Big Dave', looked up from his ham and eggs. 'Seasick, eh? No problem.' He pointed his fork. 'Go and get a can of Coke from the fridge; proper Coke, mind, none of that diet rubbish. And stick one of those bananas in your pocket.'

Colin frowned. 'Why?'

'Trust me.'

They collected their kit and walked down to the pontoon, whereupon Colin plucked up all his courage and stepped onto the dory.

'Right,' said Dave, 'drink the Coke, then eat the banana.'

Colin shrugged. 'Okay, but be prepared to see them both again in a minute.'

With Coke drunk and banana swallowed, Colin sat in the stern seat as Captain Steve opened up the engines and headed up Big Pine Key for Bahia Honda bridge. Colin waited for his stomach to reject the concoction, together with last night's beer, but the further they motored, the better he felt. In fact, by the time they were in the shadow of the bridge, he had to admit that he'd never felt better on a boat before. Not that that would be difficult, but his guts were quite settled now and even his head was losing its sense of panic. As the boat was positioned to start fishing, he sensed that he might actually enjoy himself out there.

They began to fish for the tarpon, which were migrating in large shoals through the Key. Their bait was live mullet and their tackle was robust enough to handle the sort of fish that could be hooked out there in the spring, some of which were huge. And they didn't have long to wait, because at exactly 9.30, a fish took Colin's mullet and ran away with it, tearing line off the reel as it went. Colin struck, and the tarpon immediately came out of the water and tail-walked across the surface.

'Jeeeesuuus!' cried Captain Steve. 'Hang on, Col!'

'Bloody hell!' muttered Paul.

'I didn't know they grew that big,' said Peter in a reverential tone.

As far as Colin was concerned, he was completely focused on the tackle he was using. Was the line strong enough to hold a fish like that, and did the rod have the power he would need to tire the tarpon? The skipper had already told him that if he rested, the tarpon would too, regain its strength and start the fight all over again. It might look like an oversized herring, but it would fight like a tiger, so he would have to keep up the pressure the whole time if he had any chance of landing it. Only one thing was for certain at that point: Colin didn't feel in the slightest bit seasick.

He obeyed Steve, clamped down the clutch and hung on, occasionally winning back some line but not getting the fish anywhere near the boat. Every now and again the tarpon broke through the surface and jumped, showing off its bright silver flanks in the Florida sun and the incredible power in its flailing tail. It seemed to get bigger each time they saw it, and Colin couldn't believe that he was on the other end of anything so massive.

It was over an hour into the fight that Colin became aware of two things: that they were nowhere near where they had been when the tarpon first took, and that they were collecting a sizeable armada of other angling dories around them. The boats were keeping their distance so as not to interfere, but all eyes were on Colin and his tarpon; no one else was bothering to fish until they saw the outcome of this fight.

A while later, Paul looked at his watch. 'How d'you feel, Colin?'

'Like my arms are falling off. I don't think I can take much more of this.'

Steve stood beside him. 'Look, Col, if you hand that rod over now, you'll regret it for the rest of your life. Just hang on, okay?'

Colin blew out his cheeks. 'Okay.'

'Is he tiring, d'you think?'

'Not as quickly as I am.'

Ever so slowly, Colin managed to regain line and keep it on the spool. The tarpon began to wallow on the surface now rather than jump, its tail thrashing water but not propelling it any more. Colin put more effort into pumping the rod, although whether he was pulling the fish to the boat or the boat to the fish, he wasn't sure. Whichever, the tarpon finally lay alongside, which enabled Peter and Steve to grapple hold of the fish and haul it onto the flat deck in the bows of the dory. Even so, with its body right across the boat's beam, its tail still reached into the water, a fact recorded on Paul's camera; and many others among the 30-odd boats drifting in for a closer look at the tarpon.

Paul checked his watch again. 'Two hours, 52 minutes. That's one hell of a marathon fight, Colin.'

'That's one hell of a fish, too,' said Steve. 'Biggest tarpon I've ever seen, on this or any other boat out of the Keys.'

Colin had dropped the rod and was leaning on the boat, muscles screaming with exhaustion but with an unbelievable feeling of achievement in his head. Adrenalin was coursing round his veins faster than he had never experienced before, and he couldn't speak for the moment. He was just staring down at the monstrous tarpon in front of him.

Peter held the end of the tape against the fish's tail, while Steve measured up the lateral line to its snout.

'Exactly 9 feet,' he called out, then measured the girth and did a mental calculation. 'I reckon she goes about 180 pounds.'

With that, they carefully encouraged the tarpon back into the water, where, with a disdainful flick of its huge tail, it slid away into the depths.

Meanwhile, Steve cut off the hook and handed it to Colin. It was practically bent out straight and wouldn't have kept its hold on the fish for much longer. He grinned and slapped him on the shoulder. 'You'd better keep that as a memento, Col. It's no good for fishing any more, that's for certain.'

The rest of the trip was a bit of a blur for Colin. There were more tarpon for the party, including one of 125 pounds for Peter, together with permit, jacks and some big barracuda.

But there was one more amazing incident. While fishing in one of the bays, they noticed a commotion on another boat further out to sea.

'Reel in, guys,' said Steve. 'Let's take a look.'

As they moved closer, they saw two men in the dory stabbing at something in the water with long boat hooks. On the stern of the boat was lying what looked like a lump of fish.

'That's a shark in the water!' cried Steve. 'It's attacking the damn boat, for God's sake!'

'And that's half a tarpon on the stern,' said Peter, looking through his binoculars.

It transpired that the boat had landed an estimated 80-pound tarpon and, while the captain was trying to release it, a 12-foot lemon shark had come from nowhere and slashed it in half. Even though the crew were fighting it off with the boat hooks, the shark seemed determined to grab the rest of the fish, although it finally gave up and swam away, leaving about 40 pounds of front-end tarpon on the boat, jagged teeth marks where the tail end had been ripped away.

Back in Salisbury, Peter presented Colin with a framed collage of six images of the fight and the fish, together with a scale that had fallen off its flank into the boat and, of course, the all but straightened-out hook. Apart from that hanging on his wall at home and a couple of snapshots in the shop, you would never think that Colin held the record for one of the biggest tarpon ever caught in the Florida Keys.

And if he's invited to go sea fishing from a boat these days, he's very happy to accept, just so long as he takes a can of Coca-Cola and a banana with him.

SPINNERS, ROD TOPS AND PIKE

Even a freak fishing accident didn't divert one young angler from his determination to catch a pike to be proud of.

There was a time when 6 year olds were happy enough catching tadpoles and minnows. Bertie Alexander was slightly different. It helped that he had a private lake on his doorstep but, even so, he went through the minnow stage almost without noticing it. His father and cousin fished for perch and pike, and so he was determined to be the same as them: a proper fisherman.

In fact, Bertie remembers three amazing events on the fishing front when he was 6, all happening when he was in a boat on the lake beside his home. But first, it is worth noting that Bertie, brought up in the country, had the space and, importantly, the parental encouragement to spend his time outdoors, rather than sitting in front of children's television, like most of his peers. So by the time he was 6, he was already used to cleaning out and exercising ferrets, walking dogs, and getting soaking wet and caked in mud without having to worry about what his mother would say. And of course he was, by this time, a fisherman of some experience.

He started off by watching a small float bob around the lake, occasionally seeing some action with small roach and perch. However, the problem was that he had already watched his father and older cousin catch much bigger perch and some decent sized pike by spinning for them, and that type of active fishing appealed far more. So it was not long before Bertie was sitting in the boat and throwing out ironmongery instead of bread, maggots or worms. He wore a life jacket; not that he couldn't swim, but mainly because his cousin had once been pulled into the lake when playing a pike. Or so he said!

Bertie was fishing one day with his father, out near the middle of the lake. He had caught a couple of perch on his spinner, not much bigger than the ones he had lured with worms, but now his father had hooked into something much bigger, and a pike suddenly broke through the calmness of the lake's surface. His father managed to control the fish and bring it close in to the boat, whereupon he put the big landing net over the side with one hand while he tried to coax the pike over it with his other. However, the sight of the net spooked the pike and it made a last dash for freedom. His hands full, Bertie's father couldn't control the reel as well as he needed to. The rod bent over to its maximum arc and, before he could react, the pressure became too much and the hook flew out of the pike's mouth.

With the power exerted on the line by the rod, the spinner continued flying backwards, only stopping when the rod fully loaded behind them. Then, like a well-timed fly cast, the lure came shooting forwards again. Unfortunately, Bertie was sitting right in its path this time and the treble hook smacked into him with such force that it embedded itself in the back of his head. There was a good deal of blood but, after the initial shock of the impact, it was his father who was in more of a panic about the spinner hanging from his son's head.

A quick row ashore and he was into the car and off to the local Accident and Emergency department, with the perfectly reasonable objective of having the hook surgically removed by the dedicated, professional medical staff. Except that, incredibly, the medics didn't have the right equipment to extract a big treble hook attached to a pike spinner. Instead, the consultant had the bright idea of calling up the hospital's maintenance man, who arrived with a box full of just the right kit: wire cutters, bolt crops, pliers. . .! It was not an experience Bertie was in a hurry to repeat.

Undaunted, he was back in the boat shortly afterwards, this time with his cousin, fishing for pike with big spoon lures rather than spinners. The extra weight of the spoons meant that the casts went further, and soon the two of them were having a competition over who could reach closest to the lilies. His cousin stood up in the boat to get extra height and power into his action and then threw the spoon as hard as he could towards the vegetation. Unfortunately, he obviously hadn't put as much care as usual into tackling up that morning, and the top section of the rod flew out behind the spoon towards the middle of the lake, where it landed with enough of a splash to frighten any self-respecting fish well away from the scene.

'We could row the boat over and pick it up,' suggested Bertie.

'No need,' said his cousin. 'The spoon's too big to go through the rings, so if I reel in it will bring the rod top with it.'

Whether or not the extra commotion made a nearby fish curious or it just thought that there was an outlandishly large, if rather thin, prey species splashing about, a pike came and hit the spoon in a vicious take on the surface. And because it immediately turned away, tightening the line between it and the butt section of the rod, the fish firmly hooked itself without any intervention from Bertie's cousin. He found himself fighting a very angry pike with half a rod in his hands and the other half 50 yards out in the lake.

Bertie was creased up laughing by this time, watching the rod top careering round the lake and giving a perfect pointer to where the fish was at any time. The pike even jumped a couple of times, the angle sending the rod section sliding back towards the boat, only to reverse its direction once the fish dived deeper and the angle changed back again. And because his cousin couldn't put any real pressure on the fish with only 4 feet of butt section to work with, the fight went on much longer than normal. Eventually, though, the pike exhausted itself and came meekly in to the side of the boat, preceded, of course, by the tip section. A quick twist with the tweezers released the hook and allowed the fish to swim away in a slightly more dignified manner than it had arrived.

Just a few days later, Bertie was back out on the lake with his father. He was fishing one of the big spoons again, determined to catch something that would put him in the same fishing league as the rest of his family. He had caught a few pike before, but it was only ever the small jacks which seemed to come to his lure. Even at 6 years old, a bit of a competitive edge was appearing in his psyche.

Everything started out like any other day. His father caught a couple of smallish pike and a good perch, while Bertie, who had insisted on using the biggest spoon in the box, was only feeling knocks on the line, probably from fish too small to get the spoon in their mouths. Just before tea, however, things changed dramatically.

Bertie cast towards the lily pads and began to wind in as soon as the spoon hit the water. After just a few turns of the reel handle, he felt a sudden, slamming hit that jarred all the way up his arms, as though someone had bounced a heavy weight on his line. He instinctively raised the rod and the top bent over in an alarming arch. He had hooked something quite unlike anything he had ever felt before on a fishing rod in all his six years of existence.

What happened for the next half hour or so was a bit of a haze. The power of the fish was extraordinary as it ran in all different directions round the lake, sometimes coming close to the boat, other times charging for the lily pads, stripping line off Bertie's small fixed-spool reel against a fully wound-up brake, which had surely never been designed to handle this sort of experience. He said afterwards that it was a bit like having his dog tied to the end of his line while someone threw sticks for it to go and fetch, but he absolutely refused to accept any help from his father. He was going to do this all by himself, 6 years old or not.

His arms felt like dropping off long before he finally gained some sort of control over the tiring fish. It was fortunate, perhaps, that the comparatively light tackle he was using, and his lack of brute strength, had enabled the fish to run more than a pike normally does, and so it exhausted itself a short while before Bertie did. Eventually, the fish settled into swimming round the boat a few times, before his father encouraged Bertie to exert more pressure and bring it towards the waiting net. At the very last moment, just as the net went underneath its body, the tip of Bertie's rod snapped in protest at what it was being put through.

The disintegrating tackle didn't stop Bertie's father from successfully netting the pike, and it took both his hands to haul it over the gunwale and into the bottom of the boat, where neither of them could quite believe its size.

'Am I a proper fisherman now, Daddy?'

His father ruffled his hair. 'As proper as any of us, Bertie, that's for certain!'

The fish hangs in the hall of Bertie's house, along with a brass plate recording its weight at 17 pounds, 6 ounces. He still fishes the lake for pike in winter, although he became a teenager without having caught a larger fish. At least he's managed to stay clear of flying trebles and hospital maintenance staff toolkits for the time being.

WHO NEEDS A RECORD?

When Steve Edge decided to follow the pioneers of Indian fishing and catch a golden mahseer, he began a chain of extraordinary events that led to a stunning conclusion.

In the days before one-stop-shop tour companies organised specialist Indian fishing holidays for visitors from all over the world, planning such a trip was an adventure in itself, and a slightly daunting prospect for an East End of London advertising man. However, it helped that Steve's wife was half Indian, and that she had relatives still living on the subcontinent. Telephone calls went to and fro over a period of weeks, and finally one name came to the fore. If you wanted to do anything fishing-wise in that part of the world, you needed to contact Colonel Nardhu of the Wildlife Association of Southern India.

Steve rang the number given him for the Colonel and a man speaking an Indian dialect answered the phone. This took some while to sort out, but eventually an English-speaking Indian arrived on the other end. It was difficult to understand what he was saying, as it was extremely noisy in the background.

'Colonel Nardhu?' Steve shouted.

'There is no one of that name here, Sir. This is a market stall. I don't know this man.'

Steve raised his eyebrows. 'Ah, right. I was told I could contact him here. Are you sure you don't know him?'

'Wait a minute, please.'

There was a brief pause, and he heard a more distant voice shouting out over the marketplace for anyone who might know the good colonel. Several minutes later, a new voice came down the line and yes, he knew of Colonel Nardhu and could provide contact details. And so the quest was underway.

After extended organisational negotiations across two continents, Steve finally joined a ramshackle convoy of ancient Land Rovers driving into the heavily forested valley through which the Cauvery River ran. They took all their provisions with them, including several chicken dinners still alive in their cages, which presumably surmounted the problem of a lack of refrigeration. They would live for the next week under canvas and eat in a communal area covered by an old silk parachute. This was fishing, and living, in the raw and, with its close proximity to sacred sites along the river system, was the most spiritual setting Steve could imagine. He immediately fell in love with the place and its atmosphere, and felt perfectly at ease with his local guides, two of whom, Seban and Bola, would be his main fishing ghillies.

Travelling along the valley was difficult by land, so they used a tiny coracle craft to ferry personnel and tackle from pool to pool. Despite the fast-flowing river, the coracle glided perfectly across the water surface and the ghillies were adept at coaxing it back upstream at the end of the day. It was the ideal river transport, and little time was wasted in travel during the fishing sessions.

Sport wasn't exactly frantic, although Steve landed a few small Goonch catfish and some other beautifully marked fish. He had several runs from what Seban and Bola assured him were mahseer, but it wasn't until the penultimate day that Steve managed to land a magnificent golden fish of about 30 pounds. It was the crowning glory to a fantastic week and Steve was a man content with life as he went into his final day's fishing. He had succeeded in mounting an expedition to this spiritual area virtually unknown to Western anglers, and he had the photographs of his precious golden mahseer to show for it. He was perfectly relaxed and didn't really care whether he caught another fish or not.

At that time of year, the sun went down quickly and it was quite dark by 6 o'clock. Having landed a goonch at 4.30, Steve was happy to pack away his gear and return to camp for one more night under the stars before the long journey home. However, Seban and Bola suggested one more move downstream and a final cast into a pool they hadn't fished in before, at the head of a series of shallow rapids.

The sun was already low behind the hills and the light was beginning to fade. Steve had just suggested five more minutes when the clutch on his Shimano Calcutta reel started clicking. Before he could grab the rod butt, line was shooting out towards the first of the rapids, and when he eventually managed to raise the rod tip, no amount of pressure seemed to have any effect on the fish at all. The line kept screaming through the rod rings.

'It's like having a flaming Ferrari on the end!' cried Steve, feeling completely helpless and unable to stop the run.

'How much line you got, Steve?' asked Bola.

'Six hundred yards of 30 pound.'

Bola shook his head. 'Not enough. Come on, into the coracle: we must follow this fish.'

Stepping into a coracle is a delicate operation at the best of times, but with three grown men, one with a rampaging monster at the end of his line, it seemed an impossible task. The two Indians were brilliant, though, and Steve somehow found himself kneeling down in the coracle with Saban and Bola either side and slightly behind him. They pushed off and were then at the mercy of the river's flow – and the fish several hundred yards downstream of them.

Steve went into a sort of trance, unlike any other fishing experience in his life before that point. He was concentrating completely on the fish, a feeling deep in his gut that this was something completely out of the ordinary. Saban and Bola seemed caught up in the same atmosphere, because there was silence in the coracle, except for the noise of the rapids as they sped through them.

Steve's idea of a Ferrari was very apt. The fish towed them much faster than the river's flow, so that they literally tore through the first rapid like a speedboat, through a short pool, then into a second, boulder-strewn shallow reach where the inevitable happened: the line became entangled round several rocks as the fish picked a route between them. Steve was desperate that the line shouldn't chaff on the boulders, but Saban and Bola controlled the coracle brilliantly with their flimsy paddles and managed to extricate the line around or over all the obstacles. By some miracle the monofilament stayed intact.

After the third set of rapids, they reached deeper, slower water. Here the fish decelerated and bored deeper; the two ghillies were able to paddle the coracle over the top so that Steve could regain much of his line. It was then a battle of attrition until the combination of Steve's carbon-fibre rod and Saban and Bola's boat-handling skills coaxed the fish close to the shore.

Bola hauled Steve unceremoniously out of the coracle and he finished the fight in pitch darkness on the beach, the hills starkly silhouetted against a brightly moonlit sky. At the last minute, as it was obvious that the fish was exhausted, Saban switched on his torch and there, gradually appearing out of the cloudy water, came the most magnificent, golden apparition.

'Mahseer!' whispered Bola in a hushed, reverential tone, proving that he was every bit as awestruck by the sight as Steve himself was. 'Now, that is a great, *great* fish!'

The mahseer seemed perfectly happy to be handled now, as first Bola and then Saban supported its enormous frame while they secured the recovery cord through its gills and took photographs from all angles. The fish remained calm through all this, as though it knew it was playing its part in something much more intense than merely an angling feat, and that it wouldn't be harmed in any way.

The fight had lasted almost exactly an hour and the recovery period took another 30 minutes. Steve was cradling the fish, up to his chest in water, as the cord was removed. The mahseer rolled over, its eyes momentarily staring into Steve's one last time, before it slowly sank away into the reflected moonlight and disappeared.

Back at the campsite, the post mortem took place. Saban and Bola had measured the fish at 6 feet, 7 inches, nose to fork of tail, with a girth of 48 inches.

'Okay,' said Steve, 'we know its dimensions, now what about its weight?'

Saban sighed, frowned and lent forward into the light of the camp fire. 'We have been discussing this and I think we have come to a decision. When I first held the fish, I thought it was 120 pounds.'

'But when I lifted it, I put it bigger,' said Bola, 'and the measurements prove this.'

'How much bigger?' asked a startled Steve. Despite the size of the fish, he hadn't been thinking three figures.

Saban kept frowning and looked intense in concentration. 'We have decided the fish weighed between 130 and 137 pounds.'

Steve stared at him. 'Wow! So what's the official record for golden mahseer?'

Bola smiled at him. 'Just 101 pounds, Steve. I'm sorry, you could have had the record. Do you mind very much?'

'No, Bola, just being here is amazing enough for me, thanks very much.' He lifted his tin mug of tea. 'Here's a toast to the record that wasn't!'

PART TWO

Interfering Animals

GLEN COE INFAMY

When a young boy's fishing dreams become turn into reality, the excitement of the moment can make him forget that nature gives, but can also take away.

Victor was in awe of his father and desperately wanted to impress him with his fledgling fishing prowess. He was 8 years old when the opportunity came on the family's annual Scottish holiday, although things did not turn out exactly as he was expecting, or dreaming of. In fact, he was about to experience something that would live with him in vivid detail from that day to this.

Glen Coe has a bloody past. It was here that the Macdonalds were massacred at the end of the seventeenth century in one of the most inglorious episodes of Scottish history. Back in the 1950s, when this story unfolded, Victor's parents had taken him on a walking holiday through the stunning Highland scenery around the Glen, among other things to show him where this piece of infamy took place.

His father, an angler himself, knew how keen Victor was to go fishing rather than walking or chasing history, and had given him an old bamboo rod and brass reel to take with him. On this August day, the family walked three miles into the hills to a small peaty loch, where Victor's parents left him on his own with his rod, a box of flies and a landing net. They would be back later to see how he was getting on.

Victor felt very grown up as his parents walked down the sheep track and disappeared behind a crag at the head of the loch, because this was the first time they had trusted him to be on his own so far from home. He was all fingers and thumbs with excitement as he set up the rod, but at least he remembered to grease the fly line so that it would float, just like his father had taught him. And he only needed three attempts at a figure-of-eight knot before he managed to attach the gut leader.

It was time to select a fly, and suddenly being on his own wasn't quite so easy. His father had always chosen the pattern in the past, so this was a new experience. They had gone fishing in Wales the previous year, out on a boat on Lake Vyrnwy, and Victor tried to remember what flies they had used then. He finally settled on a Soldier Palmer, because it had worked well in Wales and it seemed logical that its bright red colour would show up well in the darkly stained water in Scotland.

Victor's first casting efforts didn't amount to much, but he kept going and soon the action and timing came back to him. *Don't bring the rod back beyond 12 o'clock*: he heard his father's words in his brain, and by doing that, and wading out into the shallows as far as he could in his boots, he reckoned he was probably landing the fly far enough out to reach a fish.

He stripped the fly back at different speeds each cast, remembering what he had done on Vyrnwy, and then suddenly, out of the blue, there was a tug on the line and a swirl in the water. He struck and felt a satisfying wriggling weight on the line, which he hauled in quickly and slipped the net under a lovely 6-inch brown trout, dark flanked with beautiful vivid red spots. Brilliant! This was the first trout he had ever caught all by himself. He felt incredibly proud and couldn't wait to show it to his father.

He took the trout ashore in the net, found a suitable stone and hit it over the head. His heart was pounding with excitement, and he just wished his father would come back right now so that he could show him immediately. He gazed at the trout proudly for a few moments, then hid it beside a rock and covered it with wet grass. He went back into the water to try to catch another one.

The fish were now rising in front of him, so he had targets to aim for. He waited for a rise that was close enough, then went back to the basics of his father's casting lessons and aimed precisely at the ring left by the trout's nose breaking the surface. He missed the first few, but then he landed one exactly in the right place. There was an immediate, violent pull on the line. Victor had a brief vision of a shape swirling in the water, and then his reel was spinning out of control as the fish took off straight out into the loch, heading for deeper water.

Victor's heart was threatening to smash through his shirt by now, and he had an unbelievable adrenalin rush through his belly with the shock of that initial run. He knew this was something out of the ordinary, because he had never seen a trout behave like this on Lake Vyrnwy; it was a hugely different feeling.

A ridiculously long time seemed to pass before the fish slowed down, but it finally stopped and enabled Victor frantically to wind the little brass reel to retrieve some line. The trout came in quite easily to start with and Victor thought he had it beaten, but then it must have sensed the shallow water again and it took off on another long run. This went on for ages. Victor kept glancing across at the head of the loch, hoping to see his father coming over the crag so that he could help. Gradually, though, he sensed the runs getting weaker, and then he saw the fish splash on the surface. He remembered his father saying something about trout doing that when they were tired, so he decided it was time to try to get it close enough to land.

His first lunge with the net only succeeded in hitting the trout on the head and sending it off on another run. Victor's arms were very tired now and he wanted to get this over with, so he lost his caution and bent the rod over double to stop the fish before it reached the deep water. He managed to turn it and then bring it steadily back towards him across the surface. He guided the fish over the wooden rim and quickly lifted the net out with a great cry of triumph.

Victor kept tripping over himself in his panic to get ashore, but then dropped to his knees beside the fish and killed it with the stone. He couldn't believe the size of it: it was absolutely massive. One of the Lake

Vyrnwy trout had weighed just over a pound last year, but this was bigger, three times the size. He had caught a brown trout of at least 3 pounds, and he had done it all by himself. He just couldn't believe this was happening.

He placed the fish prominently on a flat-topped rock and then ran towards the head of the loch. A couple of curlew flew up in alarm, and Victor had a vague sight of something much larger soaring away to his right, but he was far too eager to tell his story to worry about the local wildlife for the moment. He came to the crag and stood on top, and there were his parents walking slowly. He waved his arms frantically at them, until his mother looked up and saw him. She immediately ran towards him because, as she said later, he looked as though he needed urgent help. She reached him well in front of Victor's father.

'Mummy, Mummy, I've caught this enormous. . . *massive*. . .!'

'Calm down, Victor!'

He grabbed her arm and hauled her down the loch side towards the rock and his abandoned rod and net. He pointed excitedly at the rock well before they reached it, and was just about to shout out some more about his fantastic catch when he realised that the fish wasn't there.

He left his mother and ran to the rock, thinking the trout must have fallen off. But it hadn't, it had completely disappeared. He stared in disbelief: this could not be happening to him. He was desperate for his father to see that fish, because he would never believe that Victor had caught something so big. He would just think he was lying and trying to boast, and it would be ages before he was allowed out fishing on his own again. This was an absolute disaster!

Victor started to cry. His mother tried to comfort him but he was inconsolable, and he was still sobbing his heart out when his father came up and joined them.

Victor managed to tell the story between sobs and sighs, but his tale was half-hearted. 'I know you don't believe me, I just know you don't, but it's true, all true, I *promise*. . .!'

'Victor, of course we believe you,' said his father, 'especially as I think I know what's happened.'

'What?'

'I saw a very large bird making off over the loch holding something in its talons. I think an eagle may have come down and stolen your fish.'

Victor sniffed and stared at him. It made sense, especially as he had seen a glimpse of a huge bird himself. 'But you'll never believe how *big* it was, never!'

His father put an arm round his shoulder. 'Of course I believe you, Victor. And anyway, we've got ample proof, haven't we?'

'What do you mean?'

'Look at the stone.'

Victor looked, and there was a distinct wet outline on the dry rock of where the fish had been lying. You could see where the tail had lain flat, and there was even the mark of one of the pectoral fins just behind the head.

'That looks to me like the fish of a lifetime, Victor. And you gave a golden eagle a free meal into the bargain. Now, that's a real story to tell your friends when you get back home! Congratulations – you're a real fisherman now!'

ALASKAN MELEE

Humans are not the only high-level predators at sea, but we are unique in treating fishing as a sport. Most other marine hunters need to catch fish to survive and will be looking for the easiest opportunity to snatch a meal.

Having travelled all the way home from China to England with a newborn baby when the Second World War broke out, with very little money or help of any kind, not many things in later life threw Barbara Kershaw. But even she was in for a serious shock when she realised a lifetime's ambition and went to fish for salmon in Alaska.

Barbara, now sadly no longer with us, was one of the finest women salmon fishers of her generation. She fished in Scotland from when she was a teenager until she was nearly 90, but her ambition was always to travel to Alaska and fish for the mighty Chinook or King salmon. Although she was an avid fly fisher, more than anything else she wanted to catch a King in the sea, where heavier tackle and fish baits are the norm. She was into her 80s when she finally made the trip.

Barbara flew to Anchorage, the hub of Alaskan salmon fishing safaris, and from there she took a sea plane further up the coast. On her first morning she found herself in a large bay sitting in a good-sized, comfortable boat, two rods fishing heavy outriggers down deep and using flashing lures to attract the fish in close, and then herring as bait for the main hooks.

Her rod suddenly buckled over and she reached out to grab it, but she was beaten to it by one of the boatmen, who struck into the fish, made sure it was safely hooked and then handed her the rod. To a woman of Barbara's experience this was rather irritating, and continued to be so for the entire time she was at sea. Try as she might, she was never able to beat the boatman to the rod, and so she never felt that the salmon she caught were truly hers.

However, she didn't let that get in the way of the excitement of feeling a King salmon on the line for the first time in her life, boring deep astern of the boat and pumping the heavy rod with astonishing power. She was living her dream and it was proving every bit as exhilarating as she had thought it would be.

'Er. . . I don't think it's a grilse,' she suggested to the boatman, who continued to hover too closely, as though this old woman might fall to pieces at any moment and need rescuing from the fight. 'By the way, I'm perfectly alright. There's no need to worry about me; I'm not as frail as I look.'

The salmon kept fighting, harder than Atlantic salmon in a Highland River, Barbara reckoned. It took out line on long runs, then dived deeply several times and, once she thought she had it under control near the boat, it decided to tear off under the hull so that she was convinced she would lose it by chafing the line of the keel. Gradually, though, the salmon tired and the boatman was able to net it aboard.

'Great size for smoking,' he said. 'You're allowed to kill two today. You want this one to take home?'

'Er, yes, I'd better. . . in case I don't catch another.'

'Oh, there's plenty more where that came from, ma'am!'

And more fish did come, interspersed with enjoying a stunning ringside seat as first a pod of killer whales came through the bay feeding on the salmon, and then a humpback surfaced 100 yards away and rolled around on the top, waving its great pectoral flippers like a clapping seal before swimming lazily away, no doubt in search of a shoal of herring to beat up. As well as a fishing trip of a lifetime, it was fast turning into a wildlife extravaganza that she had only ever seen before on television.

Barbara's fifth fish started very dourly after she was handed the rod. It stayed deep for some while and the extra power generated up to the rod butt told her that this was bigger than anything she had hooked thus far. She cajoled it up to mid-water, the fish still content to use its weight as its main defence until, all of a sudden, it changed tactics completely and tore up through the water column. The King exploded through the surface and jumped clear of the water, allowing Barbara to see the size of the silver bar for the first time.

'Jeees!' cried the boatman. 'That's 50 pounds of fish if ever I saw it! Don't often see 'em jump like that out here. Not that big, any 'ow.'

The fish went ballistic. Barbara had never had a salmon behave so erratically and never, of course, with that amount of weighted muscle to propel it. For three or four minutes she was completely out of control and expected the salmon to free itself at any moment. Then, just as suddenly, the chaos stopped.

Barbara was puffing heavily by this time and her arms were aching fit to drop off. If ever the boatman was wanting to intervene, now was probably the time, she told herself.

'I can't move it!' she cried. 'It's gone absolutely solid... no it hasn't, it's off again. Slow and steady... and very, very heavy. I can't stop it, the brake's useless!'

Line was being ripped off the reel against a fully wound-down brake. The rod bent over at a ridiculous angle and Barbara was convinced it would shatter at any moment. All she could do was hang on until something gave.

The boatman was leaning against the gunwale at the transom stern, staring at the line cutting through the water. 'He's coming up,' he said and glanced back at Barbara. 'Can you feel 'im?'

'Yes... I think you're right. Yes, he's definitely coming to the top.'

Then, about 120 yards behind the boat, there was a huge swirl and a large, brown head appeared on the surface. Across its mouth was the silver body of Barbara's 50-pound King salmon.

'What is it?' Barbara cried.

'It's a sea lion!' shouted the boatman. 'A bloody great sea lion's taken your fish!'

'And I bet he's eating it, the swine!' she shouted, still holding on tightly to the rod and keeping up the pressure on the salmon-cum-sea lion. 'Oh, he's let go now... I think.'

Barbara began reeling in the salmon; or part of it, at least. She could still clearly see the sea lion on the surface, chewing on what she presumed was the tail end of the fish, seeing as the head end seemed to be coming across the surface towards the boat. The fight, of course, was over.

The sea lion seemed to have finished the tail because it was now swimming at some speed after the rest of the fish. Barbara realised with horror that she was actually fishing for a sea lion with about 25 pounds of front-end king salmon as bait.

'Quickly!' the boatman shouted. 'He's catching up!'

The sea lion's attention must have been completely on the salmon and its natural defence systems were therefore down at that precise moment. It either had no idea that there were other predators around, or it had forgotten about them in its feeding frenzy.

The water exploded alongside the animal and a great, sickle-shaped fin broke surface. Barbara had a split-second vision of the top half of a killer whale's body above the water, and then its jaws closed around the sea lion in one monstrous lunge. There was an almighty swirl, a great head shake from the orca, then it sank below the surface and left just an oily, bloody patch of water where the sea lion had been.

Barbara stopped reeling, not believing what she was seeing.

'Jeees!' was all the boatman could summon up. 'I ain't seen nothing like that out here before.'

'Weeelll!' Barbara finally found her voice. 'What a to-do that was! I don't suppose I can claim my 50-pounder now, can I?' She then did what she always did in times of high excitement: she lit a cigarette, letting the boatman recover the remainder of the King salmon, unhooking it and throwing it back for whatever was under the surface to finish it off.

'I suppose I should consider myself privileged to have witnessed that,' she said, taking a deep draw on her cigarette.

'I should say! I've seen a seal take a fish off the line before, and I once saw an orca do the same thing, but I've never seen it all happen at once. Mind you, a buddy of mine up the coast seen something last year that beat even this.'

'Really? What was that?'

'He was playin' a big halibut; close on 100 pounds, he reckoned. He had it right up near the boat, getting ready to pull it aboard. Just then, from *underneath* the boat, I tell you, a damned great polar bear came up and savaged the halibut! Biggest flatfish he'd ever caught in all his life, and he goes and loses it to a polar bear. Can you believe that?'

After Barbara's experience over the past few minutes, she rather felt she could.

CROSSED LINES ON
THE LOCHY

Very occasionally, one gets the feeling that conditions are perfect for fishing. It is just unlucky, therefore, when this coincides with the natural world fighting against you and an unheard-of ghillie's blunder.

Husbands and wives who fish together make for fascinating partnerships. Women are supposed to catch more fish because of the pheromones, although that myth probably has more to do with the female willingness to listen to a ghillie's advice and follow it, rather than any gender-based advantage over their male counterparts. Some men still have hunter-gatherer's blood in their veins and are only happy when they can slap a fish onto the kitchen table for their wife to cook. Michael was happily not inflicted with the macho approach. He just enjoyed being on the river with Caroline, especially as his wife's love of the sport allowed him more fishing time than most of his friends were able to enjoy.

The couple were regular visitors to Scotland's River Lochy, a beautiful spate river on the west coast with a reputation for big grilse runs and an occasional very large salmon. On this morning there was a good, slightly coloured flow following rain over the previous few days, but the river was fining down and clearing quickly, and the portents were for excellent conditions to emerge during the day. The rise in water was almost certain to have brought fresh fish into the river, and Michael's confidence was high as he and Caroline set up their rods.

Caroline, accompanied by the ghillie, started fishing in front of Michael, although he could see them as the two pools were in sight of one another. He fished his way slowly down his water, several fish showing throughout its length at regular intervals as he waded. He had three good pulls on a Willie Gunn, but each time he lifted into the fish there was nothing. That's the typical impish behaviour of fresh-running grilse, thought Michael. They play with the tail of the fly all day long, but rarely take a decent hold of the whole thing and give the fisherman the opportunity of actually hooking something. The river needed to drop a few more inches and make the fish stop in the pools, then they might be more serious about attacking the fly properly.

He was nearing the end of the pool when he glanced up and saw that Caroline was playing a salmon. She was holding her rod up high. He could see that it was satisfyingly bent into the fish, and the ghillie was standing beside her with his net in his hand. Good, thought Michael, things are looking up at last.

He stopped fishing and watched Caroline fight the salmon. It looked a lively scrap, because every time she seemed to gain some line, the fish went off on another run. However, on its third surge upstream, towards where Michael was standing, he suddenly realised that her rod had stopped bouncing and the fish had come off. He waved his hand at her in sympathy and went back to finish off the lower end of his pool.

Michael's fly was coming across the tail when he had another pull that didn't stick. He was just cursing his luck for the umpteenth time when he felt something wrap itself round his legs. Thinking it was weed, he tried to kick it off, but it tangled round his waders even tighter, so he tucked his rod under his arm and began to unravel the spaghetti-coloured fronds.

Rather than weed, the strands turned out to be fly line, looking suspiciously like Caroline's fly line. He disentangled his legs, waded ashore and dropped his rod on the bank. He pulled at the line and recovered all the slack, but then a weight came on the other end and it began to resist. It wasn't so much a fight as an energetic wriggle, and even that didn't last long. The fish gave up and came in tamely, obviously exhausted from its previous battle with Caroline. It deserved to be released; Michael tried to revive it in the quiet water at the edge of the pool, but it obviously wasn't going to survive. He finally gave in and knocked it on the head, coiled up the spare line and headed downstream to find his wife and reunite her with her salmon.

In the lodge at lunchtime, Caroline was, of course, very grateful to have her line back, and to see the fish that had run off with it. The story of its recapture was also impressive. However, what she really wanted to know was who had tied the ruddy knot between the fly line and the backing that had failed and led to losing the salmon in the first place.

'Don't look at me,' said Michael. 'I've never had a knot come undone like that.'

Then he had a thought. The ghillie had been unusually quiet over lunch and Michael remembered that the last time they had been up on the river, they had bought the line locally and the ghillie had put it on the reel for Caroline. In that case, it was probably diplomatic to change the subject quickly and talk about the improving condition of the river and how it might affect fishing that afternoon. Ghillies did not like to be seen to have human failings.

After lunch, Michael was again fishing on his own. His pool turned a slight dogleg to the left three-quarters of the way down, so that the tail was not visible from the head. He was halfway down, fishing a shrimp pattern in much cleaner water than it had been in the morning. Salmon were moving and Michael sensed it was going to be one of those afternoons when it all went right, the kind of conditions you dreamt about but seldom experienced.

He had a couple more pulls and then a typically energetic grilse took, ripping 2 or 3 yards of line off the reel before he lifted into the fish. It felt solidly hooked and immediately set off on a long run downstream, which Michael only managed to control by the time the fish reached the dogleg. The water was shallower down there so the flow was faster, which meant that it was difficult to pump the salmon back up the pool. It stayed in the main current and, with the drag of 30 yards of line out on the water, gave the impression of being a much larger fish than Michael was sure it actually was.

Everything turned manic. The fish shot off to the right, then immediately left, after which it jumped clear out of the water, proving it was only a grilse, before haring off on a series of zigzag runs that forced Michael to give it even more line. He was now down to the backing and somewhat bemused; in all his years of salmon fishing, he had never had a fight quite like this from such a comparatively small fish.

The peculiar antics of the salmon changed yet again. It stopped dead and became a solid weight, just sitting in the current near the far bank beyond the dogleg. Michael tried to prise it closer but it simply stayed there, unmoving, for a good half minute, feeling more like a big spring salmon now than a grilse.

The fish moved again, but this time it was a much steadier, more measured run. It came left, the line sliding across the top of the water, slicing through the surface like a cheese cutter and shooting spray into the air. It kept coming and Michael started to wade downstream to recover some line, because the fish was threatening to go beyond the dogleg and that could cause all sorts of problems. He couldn't believe he was having so much trouble from a 5- or 6-pound grilse.

He wasn't able to wade fast enough to keep up with what was happening, so his line was getting perilously close to the left-hand bank that formed the corner of the dogleg. That was far too shallow for a salmon; if the fish kept going it would be on the bank, for goodness' sake!

It did keep going. Michael's line reached the corner, came clear of the water and then started sliding up the bank, cutting through a thin layer of gravel as it went. The fish had to have been in the very shallowest of water beyond the dogleg, but it still kept coming.

Michael waded as quickly as he could towards the corner, reeling in line as he went to keep in some sort of contact with the fish. When he reached the gravel beach on the corner, he saw that his line was round a tree stump and then it disappeared up the bank and under a gorse bush.

He came out of the river, still regaining line, and walked up towards the bush, now fairly certain of what must have happened.

And there, sure enough, lying down under the gorse bush and tucking into the lovely silvery grilse, was a large dog otter. Michael stopped when he saw the animal, hoping not to disturb it, but the otter had obviously seen him from a way off and had managed to rip the tail end from the rest of the fish. It stayed for a second, a pound and a half of salmon in its jaws, staring at Michael as if to admonish him for disturbing his meal after all that effort in catching it, then he turned and scurried away through the undergrowth, leaving Michael to retrieve the rest of his line and what was left of his mangled grilse.

Perhaps it wasn't going to be one of those afternoons after all. At least, not for the number of fish he was destined to land. . .

DEVERON MONSTERS

Sea trout fishing at night, surrounded by inky blackness, can do weird things to the mind and play havoc with your emotions.

The River Deveron, in Scotland's Aberdeenshire, is not the place you would immediately associate with bizarre water monsters. It is far more famous for its salmon and sea trout runs, and an excellent resident population of brown trout. Robert went for a week there every July, targeting the bright silver grilse that run the river straight off the tide at that time of year, together with a few late sea trout.

In July the weather can be bright, sunny and hot during the day, traditionally useless for salmon. However, Robert's trips to the Deveron allowed him a wonderful freedom to do just what he wanted, when he wanted. If it was bright during the day, he slept, allowing him to spend the evening, all night and early morning on the river. Normal hours of living and eating were forgotten about for that week.

This particular evening, Robert started fishing at 10 o'clock. The sun had gone down behind the trees so the river was in shade. A pod of grilse had just come into the pool and were heading and tailing in front of him. He cast his favourite evening fly, a Peter Ross tied on a treble, and felt an immediate, classic draw that took line off the reel before he struck into a solid 6-pound fish. In the next hour he landed three grilse, all silver bars fresh in from the sea, and still had time to miss several other strong pulls from running fish.

The grilse stopped taking at about 11 p.m., when darkness had properly fallen over the valley. Robert moved down to the best sea trout pool on the beat, in the deeper, quiet water above the home pool, the silhouette of the Gothic estate mansion clearly visible on the skyline above him. Cloud had moved in and the moon shone through only occasionally. It was warm, almost perfect fishing conditions.

Sea trout fishing at night can be eerie at the best of times. Above the home pool, with a wooded cliff on his left bank, Robert was acutely aware of the darkness closing in on him and standing there in the middle of a black river became very spooky. Every owl's shriek or barking fox made him more and more nervous, and wading up to his waist in water rendered him cold to his bone marrow by midnight.

He decided to give it a rest for a while so that he could warm himself on the bank with a nip of sloe gin. The final cast came slowly round in the flow, and he began a steady figure-of-eight retrieve with his left hand to keep the fly moving. Just as it came on the dangle, the rod was nearly wrenched out of his hand with a violent take from a fish almost directly downstream of him. The fish came straight out of the water and smashed back with such a commotion that it was obvious this was something different from the norm. It then ripped line off the reel and headed into the faster water at the head of the home pool.

The fight lasted a good 15 minutes. Once he had stopped that first run, Robert brought the fish back into the deeper water and managed to keep it there, letting it run round in the open but always feeling that he had some control over it. Once he felt the fish weakening, he started backing up towards the shallower water close to the bank, coaxing the fish in with him. He unhooked the net from his back, put his foot on the head and extended the handle in preparation for landing the sea trout.

Robert brought the fish into the shallows, squatted down and held out the net. He drew in the sea trout and, just as he was about to slip the net under it, he suddenly saw its outline in the water as a burst of moonlight came through the cloud. It was enormous, much bigger than he had imagined. He couldn't see it clearly, but it was considerably larger than the 6-pound grilse from earlier that evening. He was convinced the weight of the fish would go into double figures.

That hesitation, as he stared gobsmacked at the fish, was fatal. The sea trout splashed once, whipped its tail away from the net and made a sudden charge for deeper water. Robert wasn't prepared for the move, the rod bent double as the braided loop at the end of the fly line caught in the top ring, and then the leader broke above the hook. The rod sprang back, the fish was gone and Robert slumped onto his backside in the shallow water in despair. He was practically crying with frustration.

A glass of sloe gin later, shaking hands beginning to calm down, he went back into the water to try again. Almost immediately he heard the *snuffle snuffle* of an otter coming through the pool on the surface. That was no great surprise, because the Deveron had a healthy population of otters throughout its system. They were part of the delights of nighttime fishing on the river, and Robert listened to the animal until it went on up towards the pool above him.

He resumed casting and stayed in the same position for half an hour without any more takes. He was comfortably positioned in the water, his feet placed apart and dug into the gravel as a brace against the flow. Then, in the middle of a cast, he was knocked completely off balance as something smashed against his right leg and then forced its way between his feet. For a brief moment Robert was terrified, thinking that some unearthly water sprite had attacked him for daring to desecrate its river. Then there was a swirl in the water below him, at the neck of the home pool, followed by another *snuffle*, and it gradually dawned on him that the otter had swum between his legs. He stood still for a few moments, trying to regain composure, balance and confidence, and gingerly cast again, wondering what was going to happen next. This was turning out to be one weird night.

In the next 40 minutes he had half a dozen good takes and managed to land two lovely sea trout, one of 3 pounds and the other his best ever at just over 6. He took both of them ashore and laid them on the gravel bank, side by side. He kept fishing until the first dawn light began to appear in the eastern sky. Classic time for a salmon, he thought, and changed flies, feeling a mixture of emotions from his night's fishing. This time yesterday he would have settled for a 6-pound sea trout, but he couldn't get the dark outline of that other fish in the moon's rays out of his mind. He knew it would haunt him for the rest of his days.

There was a slight mist above the water as the light built. Just as he prepared to cast into the fast water at the neck of the home pool, he saw something moving downstream. It was huge, swimming across the river from right to left. Robert couldn't believe what he was seeing: the beast seemed to have horns at the front and another set in the middle of its body. It looked hideous in the mist, like something out of a fantasy horror movie. He was transfixed, his body rigid with fear as the creature slowly made its way towards the left bank. He prayed it wouldn't look his way and realise that a human was standing, helpless, in the middle of the river. If he stayed still, he might just escape unnoticed.

The monstrous beast reached the bank. Robert stared in terrified fascination as the front half appeared to clamber out first. It must be a trick of the light and the mist, but he was sure that's what was happening. And then the back half did the same and... two red deer stags stood on the bank, shaking the water out of their coats, before trotting off into the wood below the house.

Robert's heart was pumping at a clinically unhealthy rate and he felt as though his whole body was full of adrenalin. He stood there shaking, up to his chest in water, but before he could calm himself he had a sixth sense that he was being watched by someone. He glanced quickly over at the bank to where his tackle bag was laying, alongside the two sea trout. And there, standing beside them and inspecting Robert with its intense eyes and whiskered face, was the otter. They locked gazes for a few seconds, then the otter looked down at the two sea trout, deliberately reached over the smaller one and grabbed the 6-pounder in its mouth. With a last look at Robert, as though to say *thanks very much*, it dragged the fish into the undergrowth and disappeared.

Robert had the distinct feeling that the river didn't want him there at that particular moment. He wound in his line, waded quietly ashore and went back to the cottage for breakfast, wondering how he was ever going to write it all up in his game book.

INTERFERING CLAWS
AND TEETH

You may be in an exotic destination, surrounded by wonderful fish and with a state-of-the-art rod – but you don't stand a chance if the gods (and the crabs) are against you.

Mike had heard so much about bonefish, tarpon, permit and jacks that he decided to forgo two years' worth of foreign summer holidays to save enough for a week's fishing in Cuba. He agreed to join friends in a party visiting a smart lodge, with experienced guides to take them out on the flats and into the mangrove pools. Before leaving, he spent months poring over magazine articles written by experts on saltwater fly fishing, made a list of what equipment they advised he should buy, and trawled through the tackle catalogues to find the best deals from the mail-order merchants. He duly arrived in Cuba with the right clothes, reels, lines and flies for the job, together with his special purchase: a brand new design, ultralight nine-weight rod that had cost him a small fortune. In fact, he could have bought four of his normal standard fly rods for the same price. On advice from his friends, he also adopted the precaution of taking an old smuggler spinning rod with him, something he had been given years ago but seldom used. It might prove a valuable back-up, they told him, just in case anything went wrong.

Mike was an excellent fisherman under UK conditions, having caught countless trout and at least his fair share of salmon. In preparation for the Cuba trip, he had also done some saltwater training on bass, garfish and mackerel, so he was used to wading in the sea and casting at visual marine targets, even if the temperature had been slightly more conducive to neoprene chest waders than shorts and sand shoes.

The fishing began on bonefish, with his Cuban guide poling the dory along the golden flats until he found a shoal of fish. Mike then took to the water and let the guide talk him through the first few casts, homing him in on the right place to land his fly, until he became used to what a bonefish looked like in the water and he could work it out for himself. He then caught plenty of bones, easily locating them through his £200 Polaroid glasses, and becoming a dab hand at placing his crab imitation just the right distance in front of the fish and inducing the takes. And the fights were as impressive as he had been promised, with every fish screaming line off the reel as it tried to reach the safety of the open ocean. The amazing new rod coped perfectly and was a dream to fish with.

The second day they targeted permit, which his more experienced friends said were difficult, although John had caught three before and briefed Mike on how to induce a take. Again, with Carlos's expert knowledge of the flats, they found a small pod of fish in slightly deeper water than they had fished yesterday. Mike's third cast at the lead permit fell just right, and he allowed the crab to sink to the bottom before executing John's suggested twitch to bring some life to the lure. The permit, now feeding upended, reacted immediately and smothered the crab, whereupon there followed a hair-raising 15-minute fight before he brought a 20-pound fish close by for Carlos to grab by the tail.

'Man, you must think this flats' fishing's easy! All you need now is a tarpon and you've got the *slam*!'

'I want a jack as well, Carlos. I definitely need to catch a jack of some sort.'

'Okay, that shouldn't be so much of a problem. Let's try for another permit today, have a go at a tarpon in the morning, and then we'll worry about jacks and other stuff after that.'

There were no more permit and the tarpon was definitely challenging. Carlos took Mike into the mangrove lagoons, where it was easy to see the odd fish mooching around and occasionally breaking the surface, the way mullet did in tidal creeks back in the UK. Carlos nosed the boat as close as he dare and Mike cast a massive lure that even the wonder rod could only just propel far enough. The first few fish were spooked, then a couple took, jumped and immediately threw the hook, so lunchtime arrived without a tarpon. It was well into the afternoon when a small fish of about 20 pounds finally stuck and, after a couple of circuits round the lagoon, several line-shuddering jumps and generally awesome power generated back through the rod, Carlos grabbed the fish to complete the Cuban slam. There followed much hand shaking and far too much beer and rum that evening.

The next day, somewhat hung over but still basking in the glory of a slam with three days' fishing left, Mike waded the flats in search of jack. He was scanning the area immediately in front of him when he saw something shoot across the sand and stop abruptly. He peered through the rippling water and tried to make out what it was.

'Carlos, over here. What's that?'

'What's what, man?'

'That.' Rather than point with his hand, Mike stuck the top of the super rod below the surface and meant merely to point in the general direction of the beast. However, what with water refraction and a less than clear vision through last night's alcoholic haze, the tip actually touched the target.

'That's just a crab, man,' Carlos cried out, as though Mike should be able to recognise one of those by now.

However, the explanation wasn't quite quick enough. Before Mike could withdraw the rod, there was a rapid movement from the crab and a quick, solid vibration up through the carbon fibres. When he pulled it out of the water the top two inches had been broken neatly off, as cleanly as though it had been done intentionally by a specialist rod builder using a cutting tool. The tip was forlornly suspended only by the line running through the top ring.

'Ah,' muttered Carlos.

'Bastard!' shouted Mike, staring disbelievingly at his utterly wrecked pride and joy.

'That won't work now, man,' Carlos said helpfully.

'Yeah, I'd rather gathered that, thanks, Carlos. Bloody animal!'

'You got the spinner with you. Spinner's great for jack, too.'

Mike put the fly rod back in the boat, wondering whether crab nipping constituted entitlement to a new tip under the lifetime guarantee deal. Feeling distinctly miffed, he grabbed the spinning rod and followed Carlos sullenly in search of jacks, convinced that the fishing gods had turned against him because the slam had been too easy.

'There!' pointed Carlos. 'That's jack, man. Just cast over the top and bring the spinner back through them. One's certain to take.'

One did take and set off on a decent run, pulling line off the fixed spool so quickly that it sung a very high-pitched note that suggested it could break at any moment. Mike managed to control it after a while, despite having nowhere near the guts in the spinning smuggler that he had enjoyed with the nine-weight. It was fun, but it wasn't what he was there for.

The jack surfaced about 80 yards in front of him, out in deeper water.

'He looks ready, Mike,' said Carlos. 'You can bring him in now.'

Mike started to pump the jack in just under the surface, being quite firm with it so that it was deterred from any more runs out to sea. However, it was still 60 yards away when the whole surface of the water erupted, as though someone had set off a depth charge, and an enormous grey body shot out and engulfed the jack. The spinning rod was yanked down straight and very nearly torn from Mike's hands and, for about five seconds, line was ripped off the fixed spool at a ludicrous rate. He could do nothing but watch, goggle eyed, at the wake dispersing from the torpedo shape under the surface. Then the dorsal and tail fins appeared, probably 4 feet apart, Mike estimated in the short time they were visible. There was a loud crack as the rod gave way and the line broke, and Carlos had to grab hold of Mike to stop him falling over backwards.

'Bull shark!'

'Bastard shark!' Mike spat. 'The bloody thing's nicked my jack, spinner, broken the rod. . . *every damn thing!*'

Carlos stood there shaking his head. 'Bad luck, man, but it could have been worse.'

'How?'

'Bull shark can be man-eaters, and that mother was at least 8, maybe 10 feet long. If you'd been wading further out, it might have preferred you to the jack.'

'Thanks, Carlos, that's made me feel so much better!'

KODIAK BEARS AND STEELHEAD

Steelhead, the migratory form of rainbow trout, is one of the great game species and a must-catch for any globe-travelling fly fisher. The fact that bears inhabit similar country to steelhead, and enjoy eating them, adds an interesting dimension to Alaskan fishing trips.

Peter Hayes and a friend, Nigel Sturgeon, had both been to Alaska's Kodiak Island before. However, whereas Nigel had caught steelhead, Peter never had, despite catching large numbers of the various species of Pacific salmon. Interestingly, both had nearly killed themselves on previous trips in the process of trying to board small inflatable boats from shingle beaches frequented by bears. However, this had not put them off the idea of return trips, and when their friend and guide, Steve Andresen, emailed offering the steelhead trip of a lifetime, they leapt at the chance.

There are several ways to reach steelhead country. The party chose to stop off in Anchorage to visit a colleague and shop for specialist Alaskan fishing tackle at dollar prices. From Anchorage they flew to Kodiak, and from there to Steve's lodge at Port Lions. Here they boarded a Beaver float plane, which carried them at low altitude across the fantastic Alaskan landscape to the Karluk River, where they landed on a wide, flat piece of water some miles up river from the mouth.

They quickly packed all their camping and fishing gear into two 10-foot inflatables, which they navigated down the increasingly swift-flowing river, avoiding the swirling current around rocks and trying desperately to keep dry from the spray flying up from the bows. It took two-and-a-half hours, travelling through stunning scenery, before they reached Canoe Rock Hole, where they set up camp beside the river.

They were deep in tundra country. Behind them were shallow, glacial valleys covered with thin brush and willow scrub in their autumnal orange and ochre colours, and on the higher ground was a line of red and brown berry bushes, which in turn gave way to bare grey rock, the lava remains of extinct volcanoes.

It was immediately evident that bears were around, because it was obvious where they had beaten down corridors through the tall reeds that lined the riverbank. Food supplies were therefore stored well away from camp, safely concealed in bear-proof barrels.

The river cried out classic steelhead habitat, with glides, runs, riffles, islands, pools, shallow weed beds and numerous large rocks providing perfect lies for fish. The water was shallow, but with small boulders strewn around the bottom and the fast flow, wading too far out became dangerous. Peter started fishing in runs between the weeds, catching stunningly beautiful sea-run Arctic char up to five pounds, decked out in their spawning colours: dark greens, reds, orange, white, black and silver. Then the first coho salmon came to hand, a fresh-run, silver fish close to 20 pounds, and this was when things began to go wrong on the tackle front.

In his excitement, Peter laid down his rather expensive rod to deal with the fish, only for it to flap around on the shingle and then land heavily on the rod tip, snapping it cleanly off an inch from the top ring.

'Bugger!'

'I hope you got a reserve,' said Steve.

'Yeah, but only one.'

'Better be careful, then. These steelheads fight like hell, yer know!'

On the second day Peter hooked and lost four big fish, and then finally landed a magnificent fresh 27-inch steelhead, silver flanked with iridescent pink flashes. As evening approached he hooked a big steelhead in front of Canoe Rock, which fought him for ages, continually leaping and showing off its freshness in the dwindling light. However, with a steep bank behind, it proved difficult to land and the fish managed to free itself at the last moment. It would prove to be the biggest steelhead of the whole expedition, but it went unmeasured.

Bad luck with his tackle continued to dog Peter, as the braking system on his supposedly top-grade reel worked only intermittently. Problematic tackle didn't stop the third day being a huge success, with Peter landing another five steelhead. The drag setting would give way during the fight and then unexpectedly bind again, with the result that several fish were bounced off by the sudden jolt. Such are the perils of fishing hundreds of miles out in the wilderness, with little room in bags for spares or repair kits.

The third day was a great success, however, with Peter landing another five steelhead. As all the fish were returned alive, size was calculated using the standard formula for salmon and trout: nose-to-tail length multiplied by girth squared and divided by 700. As a result, Peter's largest fish that day went 31 inches and 10 pounds in weight, while Nigel landed a 33-inch fish that would have been at least 12 pounds.

The climatic variability of Alaskan Tundra in autumn was given its full range during the following 24 hours. There was 14 degrees Fahrenheit of frost that night, which, apart from being freezing cold for campers, produced a morning water temperature of only 36 degrees, which then warmed by a staggering 10 degrees during the day as the air temperature soared into the 70s. By mid-afternoon Peter was fishing without a shirt, but the only steelhead he hooked promptly ran out 150 yards of line before jumping and throwing the hook.

Despite the intensity of the fishing, Peter always had half an eye for the wildlife. Bears had been wandering up and down the river fairly regularly during daylight, although they mercifully kept away at night.

Peter had seen one family group in particular roaming the riverbank, consisting of a sow and two well-grown, 'teenager' cubs, although the mother had kept her offspring away from the campsite. He had even broken off from fishing for a while to film the animals, a shotgun ready in one hand just in case, while operating a rather shaky camera in the other.

That Thursday afternoon, the bears had passed by on their down-stream journey around teatime, heading probably for the river mouth that, although some 15 miles away, would still be within their foraging territory. However, the fishing camp a mile below had other ideas, and made such a racket with shouts and whistles that not only did Peter hear them, the bears did an about turn and came waddling back. They arrived on the opposite side of the river just as Steve was grilling a coho for supper.

The male cub stopped and sniffed the air, but was encouraged to keep going by his mother and so the group disappeared upstream. However, as the light faded, another anglers' camp turned the bears round yet again and sent them back downstream, only this time they were on Peter's side of the river and the male cub, probably fed up with humans interfering with his foraging, very definitely now had grilled salmon in his nostrils.

Peter, Nigel and Steve chased the cub away twice, but the bear climbed the steep bank and defiantly stayed his ground some 30 yards from the dinner tent, continually sniffing the fragrance of cooked salmon on the air. He was obviously intent on another attempt at stealing the fish, so the three anglers formed a defensive line: Steve with a pump-action shotgun loaded with slugs to kill, Peter with another gun loaded with cracker shells and Nigel holding the boxes of spare cartridges for both. In front of them were the three bears, the male cub aggressively in the lead. At this point, obviously deciding that the salmon was rightfully his, he charged.

'Shoot him, Pete,' said Steve quietly.

Peter waited a fraction longer, then fired at 10 yards' range. The cracker shell hit the bear slap on the nose, bounced off as intended, fell into the grass and exploded like a Thunderflash. The bear skidded to a halt, spun round a hundred and eighty degrees and galloped out of the camp as fast as his legs would carry him.

"Hell," said Steve. "That bear must have been doin' thirty miles an hour on the way in." Peter laughed nervously, loading another cracker shell into the breach. "Yeah, but I reckon he was doing forty on the way out! Let's hope he's learnt his lesson."

The bears vanished into the undergrowth and showed no signs of returning. Even so, Peter spent a long, nervous and sleepless night listening out for prowling predators, not to mention his companions' carefree snoring. As soon as dawn broke, he gingerly stuck his head out of the tent and there, sure enough, were the three bears again, just 200 yards from the camp catching field voles.

'I guess a bear's gotta do what a bear's gotta do,' he thought ruefully, mimicking Steve's voice in his head. He just prayed that vole hunting would keep the animals occupied for the rest of the trip so that he could concentrate on the steelhead, and catch up on much needed sleep.

There was plenty of other tundra wildlife to go with the bears. They saw several bald eagles, one so close to the boat that the party drifted by underneath the branch on which it was perched. There were foxes, one of which was already turning into its silver winter coat, and three Sitka blacktail deer, including a young animal crossing the river in front of Peter while he fished. To cap it all, a family of voles nested under the boat, although luckily the bears did not discover them, otherwise the rubberised transport home might have been shredded.

But Peter's abiding memory from the week, apart from the fantastic fishing, the scenery and the utter wildness of the country, was the low-octave growl of the mother bear coaxing her cubs to follow her, and the louder, angry roar of a boar grizzly some way upstream, reacting to another camp's Thunderflash dissuader. However marvellous it was to see brown bears in the flesh like that, so close and in their natural environment, the 12-hour Alaskan nights spent wondering whether Wiltshire fisherman might be on the predators' menu played on the nerves somewhat by the end of the week.

'Would you come back?' asked Steve as they watched the Beaver taxi towards them.

'Like a shot,' replied Peter without any hesitation, 'although I might just bring a few more cracker shells with me next time!'

PART THREE

Ghosts

MAIRE'S COTTAGE

The loughs in the west of Ireland are remote places now, but were even more so in the years between the two world wars. Remoteness can lead to very strange happenings, particularly in bad weather.

Added to the eerie emptiness of the Celtic landscape, the weather has always played a pivotal part in fishing these massive waters. Coming in from the Atlantic ocean, it can change dramatically in a short time and catch out the unwary fisherman, especially those afloat.

History does not relate which lough Charles Cuthbertson was fishing. We do know that it was his first trip to Ireland, and that he was so enthusiastic about his trout fishing that he was prepared to ignore the pessimistic weather prognosis from the boatman he had hired for the week. After two successful days' fishing, the boatman refused to take

Charles out on the Wednesday, saying that an Atlantic storm was on its way and would turn the lough into a maelstrom by the afternoon.

Charles did not want to lose even a few hours' precious fishing, so he promptly loaded his tackle into the boat and started the Seagull engine. He motored away on his own to begin a drift in a bay along the north shore, where they had caught some lovely trout the day before. He was soon catching fish and became completely focused on the trout, so that, without really being aware of it, he drifted further and further out from the bay and into the main body of the lough. He was conscious that the wave height was gradually increasing, but only because the extra movement was helping him attract more fish to his top dropper. He sensed no danger at that point.

By the time Charles fully appreciated the deteriorating conditions, all landmarks had disappeared; the increasing wind had driven low cloud in from the west and it had begun to rain. He was mildly concerned now and so he stowed his rod in the bottom of the boat and started the Seagull, then turned the boat into the wind and opened the throttle. Almost immediately, a wave came over the bows and soaked his fishing bag, then another quickly followed. To stop shipping water, he had to close the throttle until the boat only just had steerage way, so he resigned himself to a long slog home against the elements.

The weather closed in very quickly and the rain became much harder. He was wearing an oiled jacket, but his trousers were soon soaked. He sat there, shivering, until his worst fear happened: the engine spluttered and died, almost certainly having run out of fuel. The boat swung round, beam on to the waves, and began rolling wildly, so that he couldn't even try to restart the engine. He dragged himself to the middle seat, put out the oars and managed to turn the boat's bow into the waves. He didn't have a hope of rowing against the weather, but he had enough knowledge of boats to know that if he could keep her head into it, he could let the waves carry him in relative safety until he reached the downwind shore.

Charles lost track of time. The experience became nightmarish, his arm muscles screaming from the effort of keeping the boat straight and his whole body now soaking wet and freezing. The low cloud had merged into darkness as night closed in and he felt terribly alone and scared. Eventually, he reached the point where he thought of giving in, letting the boat come beam on to the weather and accepting the inevitable. At least it would be over quickly.

Suddenly, the boat hit the bottom with an almighty thump, then seemed to bounce onto the next wave and crash down onto solid ground. It swivelled round in a complete circle and tipped over violently as the next wave hit it, throwing Charles out in the process and hitting him a glancing blow on the head as it landed, upside down, beside him. He lay on the ground, too far gone even to feel relief that he was finally off the water.

Some time later he opened his eyes and looked around him. His heart leapt. Through the darkness and the murk he could see a flickering light, and he convinced himself it must be from a nearby house. He pulled himself to his feet and staggered towards the light. There, sure enough, was a small cottage with a lantern in the window. Charles collapsed against the door and rapped its iron knocker as loudly as he could.

The door opened and he fell across the threshold.

'Oh, you poor dear!' said an old woman. 'You look as though you're perished. Come in by the fire.'

Charles nodded and smiled his thanks at her, then lurched across and sank to his knees in front of the open grate.

'You'll be wanting some tea,' she said, 'and I have some stew on the hob. Here, now, take those clothes off and I've a blanket you can wear until they're dry.'

'You're ... too kind,' he stammered, his teeth chattering uncontrollably.

'Nonsense! I often help the fishermen off the lough. Old Maire never turned one of you away when you needed help.'

Charles slowly revived as his body began to dry and warm, and the stew tasted as good as anything he could remember eating. The old woman fussed kindly around him to make sure he was comfortable and soon, utterly exhausted, he was fast asleep, curled up on the floor in front of the fire.

When Charles woke, it was quite dark. He felt better, although still cold and weak. However, he was now conscious that people at the hotel must be worried about him. He felt in the dark for his clothes; they were still uncomfortably damp, but he put them on and tiptoed to the door. He didn't want to disturb Maire, who was obviously still asleep somewhere. He would get the hotel proprietor to drive him out here later on, so that he could thank her properly for her kindness and bring her a gift of some kind.

He went outside and shut the door, noticing that the hinges needed a good oiling and thinking perhaps he could do that for Maire that afternoon. He searched around in the dark until he found an obvious track leading away from the cottage. He knew that a road skirted the northern bank of the lough, and he could see a slight lightening in the dawn sky over to his right showing him where east was, so he had a natural compass to guide him. Thankfully, the rain had stopped and the wind had at least lost yesterday's intensity.

Charles reached the road after half an hour's brisk walk. He turned left and began the long hike back but, just as the sky began to lighten properly, a car appeared from the direction of the hotel. It stopped and the hotel proprietor, Sean O'Reilly, stuck his head through the window.

'Mr Cuthbertson, thank God we've found you! We thought you were at the bottom of the lough. Get in man, get in.'

Charles climbed into the passenger seat and they began the drive back to the hotel.

'Where did you spend the night?' O'Reilly asked.

'Old Maire took me into her cottage and looked after me.'

The car screeched to a halt so abruptly that Charles nearly hit his head on the windscreen.

'What did you say?'

Charles told his story to an increasingly incredulous O'Reilly. When he had finished, the man said nothing, turned the car round and drove back the other way. Charles asked him a couple of times where they were going, but the proprietor remained silent and stony faced.

They reached the track and turned down towards the cottage, the car bouncing around on the potholed surface. Soon the cottage came into view and O'Reilly stopped the car beside it, whereupon it became glaringly obvious to Charles that something was wrong. This was no longer a snug, waterside cottage with smoke coming welcomingly out of the chimney, but a dilapidated, unlived-in ruin with half its roof missing.

When they creaked open the door on rusted hinges, the inside was just as derelict. With daylight now coming through the broken windows, Charles saw rubbish lying around on the floor and a small pile of wood by the fire grate, in which were some dead embers.

'Is this where you stayed last night?' asked O'Reilly.

Charles was staring around him, bewildered. 'There must be some mistake. There's another cottage down here, surely?'

'No more cottages, this is the only one. And no one's lived here since Maire died these 30 years past.'

'Don't be ridiculous, man, I saw her with my own eyes. She gave me rabbit stew!'

O'Reilly walked over to the grate and felt the embers. 'They're still warm, so you did stay here last night, that's for certain, but not with Maire. I think you must have been suffering from hypothermia or something and you were hallucinating.'

Charles stared at him, not taking this in at all. 'But. . . but. . .'

'We always keep some wood and kindling and matches here, just in case anyone gets caught out on the lough or wants a dry place to have lunch. You must have started the fire yourself. The rest was in your imagination, Mr Cuthbertson, believe me!'

Charles slowly nodded his head. That must have been it: he had managed to find his way here and light a fire, but everything else had been a dream.

O'Reilly put an arm round his shoulder and guided him out through the door. 'Let's get you back to the hotel, where you can have a bath and a decent breakfast. You'll feel better then.'

Charles walked back towards the car. Then he stopped dead in his tracks and stared at O'Reilly. 'If I dreamt all this, how did I know Maire's name?'

O'Reilly had a weird look on his face. 'That's the bit I have no answer to, Mr Cuthbertson, no answer at all!'

SEA TROUT AND
STANDING STONES

Night fishing for sea trout can be an eerie experience at the best of times. Link that to the atmosphere and ancient history of the Scottish islands, and you have all the ingredients for a classic ghost story.

L och Bharp, on the island of South Uist in the Outer Hebrides, off Scotland's west coast, is a supernatural place on the brightest of summer days, let alone as night draws in. The whole area is surrounded with relics of ancient history, such as the standing stones erected thousands of years ago, a local Stonehenge. But it is the Norse influence, beginning back in the dark ages, that lies behind this particular story. The Vikings sailed here from their Scandinavian homeland, made landfall and settled on the island. It must have been an attractive proposition more than a millennium ago, with the abundance of fish in freshwater lochs and the sea to sustain the invaders throughout the year.

South Uist still has some of the finest wild brown trout fishing in the world, especially among the limestone machair lochs, which produce such beautifully proportioned, fat and healthy fish. This is the primary reason anglers from far afield visit the island, together with the sense of wilderness it evokes: the place has survived human interference since the Vikings held sway there.

The sea trout on South Uist are as famous as the brownies and they will take the fly freely during daylight, both in estuaries and inland lochs. But in August, when this story unfurls, the best time to catch sea trout in freshwater is at dusk, with the glare leaving the water as the light fades away. And Loch Bharp is just the place to be at twilight if you're an avid sea trout angler. At least, it is if you're a visitor to the island and don't know any better.

This particular evening, a lone angler decided to leave the other members of his party after dinner at the Loch Boisdale Hotel and visit Bharp. In an effort to keep his identity under wraps, we will simply call him Peter. He waded into Bharp from the east bank, the wind from his left side to help his casting, and the last of the dwindling light out in front.

He told his friends afterwards that he had been optimistic about the fishing because the weather was so good. It was balmy, with the southerly wind creating a slight ripple on the loch's surface. He felt perfectly comfortable, even though he was wading up to his waist in the shallows, and he was at peace with the world as he began to fish. His optimism was rewarded with a regular succession of small sea trout coming to his Bibio bob fly. What could be better, or more tranquil, than to be on Bharp that night, enjoying classical sea trout fishing in near perfect conditions?

He was concentrating so hard that he was only vaguely aware of the dwindling light turning to night. Even in August, the daylight is slow to fade in the Outer Hebrides, lingering for longer than it does further south. Peter had no need to change his fly so the darkness did not impede his fishing, and the wading was so easy close to the bank that there was no problem with not being able to see into the water.

The first he knew that anything untoward was happening was when the temperature dropped dramatically, even though there was now plenty of cloud cover and the wind remained in the south, so should still have been a warming influence. Peter was an experienced sea trout fisherman and knew instinctively that nothing meteorological should be causing the sudden change in conditions. Whether through this realisation or some inner sense that something very strange was about to take place, he felt the hairs on the back of his neck stand on end and a shiver of adrenalin dart down his spine.

Peter looked up and across to the other side of the loch. In the darkness, in the middle of that wilderness surrounding Bharp, there should have been nothing more than the silhouette of the landscape against the western sky. There certainly should have been nothing remotely linked to human activity, because he was certain that he was the only one out after sea trout, and there was nothing else for anyone to be doing there at that time.

A line of flickering lights was moving slowly across the horizon. Peter said later that, although he was a long way from what was happening, he immediately had the impression that people were walking very slowly from left to right, each holding a torch to light their way. Not a modern torch with battery light, but an old-fashioned one lit by flame. He also knew that, because he was aware of the topography over there, the line of lights was heading in the direction of the standing stones. He had a vision of a line of figures, perhaps olden-day monks in habits and cowls, walking towards that ancient site. Whether that was actually happening he didn't know, but that was how his imagination saw it.

The air was not only freezing now, but held an intense atmosphere that was closing in on Peter with a blackness that was much darker than the night around him. He stood there rooted to the spot in rapidly increasing terror, the only thing visible to him now being the line of lights moving across the skyline. And then a deeply unnerving feeling welled up into his guts that he was not welcome on Bharp. The comfortable environment he had waded into at dusk had been blown away. Instead, and as ridiculous as it seemed out there in the middle of nowhere, he felt that he was intruding where he had no right or business to be, and that he was being told by some unknown authority to leave immediately.

Peter turned and fought his way through the water for the shore, tripping over boulders and slipping on gravel in his panic to get away from the place. Several times he fell to his knees, soaking the upper part of his body and bruising his legs, but the pain made no impression, such was his manic determination to get away from the loch. He scrambled up the bank, dived into his car and drove at a ludicrous speed all the way back to the hotel.

His friends had been at the whisky by the time he staggered into the bar, and there were a few other visiting anglers and some of the locals with them. Despite the malty haze in his head, one of the party, who later related this story, said that one look at Peter was enough to realise that something dreadful had happened. He was white as a ghost and his hands were trembling uncontrollably. The fact that he hadn't taken off his waders before entering the bar and that the top of his shirt was soaking wet suggested he was in a high state of distress.

Peter finally managed to string enough words together to give everyone an idea what had taken place out on Bharp. His friends mostly greeted the tale with alcohol-fuelled ribaldry, but not so the locals. One of the ghillies thrust a large glass of whisky into his hand.

'Drink that, Peter, I reckon you need it. You see, you don't stay out on Bharp after dark. Everyone round here knows that.'

'Wh ... hhy?'

The ghillie shrugged. 'It's just something you don't do.'

'Who are those ... people out there? I take it they *are* people?'

The ghillie nodded. 'Yes. Or at least we think they were, once.'

'Ghosts? You think I've seen ghosts?'

The ghillie looked serious. 'Let's just say I think you've seen something unearthly.'

The story has no definite ending, because no one has ever dared go close enough to the standing stones to find out what goes on there after dark. The locals swear it has nothing to do with the living and, anyway, Peter says that it was not so much the visual aspect of the incident, but the intense menace of the atmosphere out on the loch that scared him the most. He was convinced that no living person could ever have conjured that up.

And so, whether the torch carriers were ancient builders of the stones, pagan Norsemen, druids or early Christian monks, no one can say. But what they will tell you on South Uist is that, as good as the sea trout fishing may be on Bharp as the sun goes down, don't be stupid enough to be there!

KING HENRY'S HORSEMEN

Ghost stories told during daylight may seem trite, but they can take on a much more frightening realism once darkness falls over an ancient wooded riverbank.

The area surrounding Hampshire's Beaulieu River, on England's south coast, is steeped in mysterious history. Ancient woodland and human settlements from the earliest of times have left their mark on the landscape, and today the place can still feel uncomfortable, especially along the riverbank at night. Then there are the ruins of Beaulieu Abbey, where visitors to the National Motor Museum sometimes see monks tending the gardens, only to be told by the staff that the last monks left hundreds of years ago. It is the sort of place you expect to see a ghost round every corner or some monstrous gargoyle in each nook or cranny. And so, in retrospect, it probably wasn't all that clever for Andrew and Chris to visit the abbey during the day . . . but we're getting ahead of ourselves.

A great friend of Andrew's knew the river well, especially the bottom end, near its mouth. It is an isolated place and he had been on his own during the previous week, hunting the sea trout that, unusually, will take freely during daylight, provided you fish for them in the right way. They don't want large flies, but they will come to a small nymph, even a dry fly sometimes. Andrew's friend had caught some beautiful fish up to 6 pounds, but there was one sea trout that had been driving him mad.

'It's the biggest fish I've seen in the Beaulieu, or any other river, come to that. He came at the fly three times, but turned away at the last second each time. He's too canny for me, at least in daylight. He might take a fly at night, though.'

'When are you going after him, then?'

'I don't fish the Beaulieu at night, Andrew; too bloody creepy for my liking. No, I'll leave the fish to you, but you'll owe me one if you catch him.'

So the plot was hatched and Chris agreed to accompany Andrew on the quest. They went down to the lower river in the morning, when the tide was just flooding, and did a thorough recce. There were a number of small sea trout shoals lying against the far bank, some with large fish among them, although not the sort of size they had been told to expect. Then, just as the tide was stirring up the silt, they saw half a dozen fish lying close together in the shade of a line of bushes.

'Jeeesuus!' Chris whispered. 'The smallest one must be 8 pounds!'

'What about that big bugger?' breathed Andrew.

'15? 18?'

'I was going to say 20. It's bloody enormous, whatever weight it is.'

'It won't be easy, will it?'

'We'll have to choose the right time and then stalk it.'

Andrew looked around him at the landmarks. There weren't many to go on, apart from the fencing that kept the cows out of the river. There was a stile that they should be able to find in the dark, and they could pace it out from there to where the fish were lying, so they would know roughly where they were.

'Okay, what do we do for the rest of the day?'

'Visit the Motor Museum and the abbey,' suggested Chris.

They spent the morning inspecting cars, then went into the abbey and house in the afternoon. There was a guide in the house talking about the ghosts that were seen around the estate, even sometimes on the river. The Beaulieu was an important trading highway in the old days and the monks would use it to transport some of their agricultural produce, and to bring in wines and spices from the continent. They were still seen on the riverbank apparently, carrying barrels over their shoulder or sacks of corn, no doubt looking for spectral ships on which to load their cargoes. And finally, most chillingly of all, there was a story about a group of King Henry's horsemen still galloping through the forest, riding down the fleeing monks after the sacking of the abbey during the dissolution of the monasteries.

This was fine while they were listening to amusing stories in Beaulieu House designed to impress the tourists and visitors. Andrew and Chris even laughed about them in the pub over supper, but it became a different story when they walked down the river as dusk was falling. To add to the spookiness of the isolated place, the breeze was gently rustling the trees, making it sound in Andrew's imagination as though the ghosts were whispering to one another about these foolish fishermen daring to venture into such an unholy place as night was closing in. Enormous sea trout suddenly didn't seem quite so enticing after all.

Then they were walking through the ancient woodland and it became very dark indeed. A tawny owl hooted just above them, making Andrew jump half out of his skin, and something flew straight across in front of him; probably a nightjar, but it could just as easily have been an impish sprite sizing him up. Nervous butterflies were fast turning into terrified snakes slithering around his stomach. He expected Henry VIII's cavalry to appear at any moment and mistake him for a monk.

They finally reached the stile that led into the sea trout field, at which point Andrew tried to put a dispassionate air on proceedings and start thinking fish. He turned to Chris. 'I don't think we'll try the big one just yet. Let's fish here for half an hour until it's pitch black, then we'll walk down and see if we can nab him.'

Andrew started fishing, casting a large silver stoat's tail into the inky blackness of the Beaulieu. There wasn't much flow at this point and he slowly figure-of-eighted the line back, keeping the lure moving at a constant rate. But it was all robot-like and mechanical, with no real thought as to where the fish might be holding at that moment. He was far too aware of the forbidding darkness surrounding him, and he decided to give it a rest for the time being and try to compose himself on the bank before the main onslaught began.

He sat beside a willow tree with his back to the fence. He carefully uncovered his illuminated watch dial: it was just after 11 o'clock. Another 15 minutes and he would find Chris, then they could stalk the monster. He had already decided to give his friend first crack. Andrew was quite happy to play ghillie tonight and allow Chris the chance of the fish of a lifetime.

With nothing to do but stare out over the river, the darkness began to play tricks on him. Every movement of a branch in the breeze was a monk with a barrel over his shoulder, and when another owl, or perhaps the same one, screeched close by, he was convinced the horsemen were coming for him.

Then there was the most horrendous scream he had ever had the misfortune to experience. It was only just along the bank and he knew instantly that something hideous must have happened to Chris. He recognised his voice only too well, albeit amplified in a violently rasping, throat-strangling sort of way. This was followed by a low, continuous moan, as though his friend was in utter turmoil over some godforsaken event that had overtaken him. Then, most dreadful of all, the unmistakable sound of galloping hooves going away over the field towards the forest.

Andrew's blood froze; in fact, he was so petrified, he couldn't move. His imagination saw Henry's horsemen riding through the night, their leader's sword still in his hand, Chris's blood dripping down the blade onto the hilt. He had died an evil death, for dead he must be; the moaning had stopped and all was now eerily silent once again.

Andrew finally plucked up the courage to go over and take a look at the crime scene. He stood up and shone his torch. No need to keep hidden now; sea trout were the last thing he was worried about. He crept along the bank and the beam of light caught the hunched-up figure of Chris, his back still leaning against a fence post beside the field. Then, oh joy! He moved, his arm coming up to cover his eyes against the glare of the torch.

'What the hell happened?' cried Andrew.

Chris's face was white as a ghost and the expression on his face told its own story: he had just received the biggest fright of his life. His mouth opened, but nothing came out. He just pointed despairingly behind him.

Andrew shone the torch over the fence and two cows stared back at him, their eyes shining bright in the torch beam. What had happened was that Chris had decided to have a quick nap before taking on the leviathan fish, forgetting that there were cows in the field and that cows are highly inquisitive animals. He had been woken by one of them literally breathing down his neck from above. The scream and moans had been his, while the galloping hooves belonged not so much to Henry's ghoulish riders as to the startled cow fleeing in terror from the howling human.

Needless to say, the monstrous sea trout remained uncaught. Hopefully its offspring still run the Beaulieu River to this day.

THE VIKING'S LOVER

There has to be a good reason why ghillies won't land on a beautiful island, and why sea trout don't seem to take a fly in its vicinity.

Loch Maree, on Scotland's west coast, was arguably once the finest still-water sea trout fishery in Europe. Hopefully it will be again, if some of the environmental problems that caused its demise can be reversed. But back in its heyday, people would make the annual pilgrimage up to the loch from all over the world, staying at the equally famous Loch Maree Hotel, and rarely were they disappointed with sport that was consistent for decades.

Maree was also the Scottish landfall for the art of dapping. Established as a great way of taking sea trout on the big Irish loughs, it proved just as effective on Maree. This was one of the attractions for husband and wife anglers John and Veronica, who loved the loch so much that they made annual visits for many years and, whenever the breeze was strong enough, they dapped. At lunchtime each day, they would either land on the shore if that was close enough, or one of the islands dotted around the loch. The routine of the week rarely changed and it was an idyllic fishing holiday for them and the countless other visiting anglers.

However, one island on which they never landed was the largest in the loch, Isle Maree. They didn't initially register that their ghillie seemed to stay clear of the place; there were more than enough fish to be taken elsewhere, so it was never an issue. They just assumed that fishing around Isle Maree wasn't good enough to bother with. It was only on one particular day, when the morning had been great for dapping but the wind was dying away in the afternoon, that they realised something wasn't quite right with the island.

They had some good sea trout in the boat from the morning session, Veronica in particular having excelled herself dapping a Goat's Toe. Now they happened to be close enough to Isle Maree for John to notice that there were fish rising just off its shoreline.

He glanced at the ghillie. 'David, there must be a buzzer hatch or something going on over there. Let's take a look.'

'No point, they'll only be small fish.'

'They look like decent rises to me. It must be worth a cast?'

It was obvious that David wasn't enthusiastic, but he set the boat to drift down along the island's shoreline. There wasn't enough wind to dap, so they fished teams of traditional flies and, soon after starting, Veronica hooked a big sea trout. The fight went on for a good 10 minutes but, just as the boat drifted level with the southern tip of the island, the fish jumped and threw the hook.

'Damn! That would have been my best ever!' Veronica stated vehemently.

'Don't worry, there's plenty more fish here,' said John. 'Look, they're rising all over the place.'

But try as they might, neither of them could get any reaction from the fish. It even got to the point where they were convinced the sea trout were actually swimming round their flies. They were rising all right, but they didn't seem to be feeding on anything; there was no hatch of fly. They were behaving very peculiarly.

'This is flaming odd,' said John after a while. 'I would have bet my last shirt we would have taken fish out of this shoal.'

'Always the same off this island,' muttered David. 'I've got no confidence in the place.'

'As the fishing's died off, shall we land on the island and have a look round?' suggested Veronica.

'Sorry, I don't go there,' David declared.

'Why ever not?' she asked. 'It would be terrific to land and have a look round while we're here. Apparently it's lovely.'

'Absolutely no way! We just don't go on that island. Look, we might as well call it a day now and get you back to the hotel for dinner. We can have an early start in the morning to make up for it.'

John raised his eyebrows at Veronica. 'Oh alright, David, if you say so.' The fishing didn't look as though it would pick up before dusk anyway, so they weren't missing much. However, he was fascinated to know more about this obsession David seemed to have with Isle Maree.

Back at the hotel, they sat David down in the Ghillies' Bar with a glass of beer and were soon joined by one of the other ghillies, Kenny. After some talk about the day's fishing and prospects for tomorrow, John bought another couple of rounds of drinks and, when he thought they were suitably relaxed, brought the conversation round to the loch's islands.

'Look, you two, what's all this business with Isle Maree? Why won't you land there?'

Kenny laughed. 'You've no chance of getting David even close to that place, let alone on it!'

David scoffed at his friend. 'Okay, so you'll take 'em out there tomorrow?'

'Ah, I didn't promise that.'

'No, I bet you didn't, and you won't, neither.'

'Come on,' Veronica encouraged, 'you've got to tell us now.'

David glanced at Kenny. 'It's just spooky there, that's all.'

'Why?'

David took another mouthful of beer and wiped his mouth with his hand. 'Okay. Well, it goes back 1000 years or more, to when the Vikings ruled here. A bloke called Prince Olaf was a Norwegian warlord who did pretty much what he liked in these parts. He used to visit a hermit who lived on Isle Maree and ask for advice about his battles and whatnot. Legend has it that old Olaf fell in love with a local girl and wanted to marry her, but because he lived on a ship with his men, he couldn't expect her to go there with him. So the hermit suggested he build a tower on Isle Maree and live in it with the girl.'

'They lived happily ever after and then died?' suggested Veronica.

Kenny shook his head and chuckled. 'You couldn't be more wrong.'

'Olaf stayed with her for a few honeymoon months,' David continued, 'but then his men got twitchy and persuaded him to go off on a pillaging raid down the coast. While he was gone, his new princess started getting doubts about whether Olaf really loved her; you know, she was worried he was happier fighting with his men than being married to her. So she hatched a plan for when he came home, to see whether he really did love her or not. As soon as his boat came into the loch from the River Ewe, she got onto her barge and lay down on a sort of funeral pyre, as though she was dead, and her servants covered her body in a shroud so that it looked authentic. Then they went out to meet Olaf's longboat, the princess waiting under the shroud to see what Olaf's reaction would be when he thought she'd snuffed it.'

'Sounds a bit Romeo and Julietish,' suggested Veronica.

David nodded. 'Aye, something like that. Olaf jumped onto the barge and threw back the shroud, and of course he thought his princess was dead, so he let out a huge cry of. . .'

'You've forgotten the bit about his temper,' Kenny came in. 'Olaf was supposed to have been a real fiery Norseman who would go crazy if something provoked him.'

David nodded. 'Yeah, that's right. Well, by all accounts, he must have properly loved this girl because he was immediately gripped with uncontrollable grief. Before she could react, he drew his dagger in a fit of rage and plunged it into his heart, so that was him done for. When the princess realised what she'd done, she pulled the dagger from Olaf and stabbed herself, although she didn't do such a good job. She made it back to the island, where the hermit, a druid holy man, blessed her, then she died.'

'Wow, what a story!' cried Veronica. 'And were they buried out on the island? Is that the problem?'

Kenny nodded. 'Aye, they're still out there all right. They were buried feet to feet, so that they could spend eternity looking at each other, and they were surrounded by holly bushes, which were holy trees to the ancients. That's why there's so much holly on the island now.'

'Can you still see the graves?'

'Aye. They're stone slabs with different designs of cross etched into each one. You can still see the pile of stones where the tower used to be as well.'

'And you never go there?' asked John.

Kenny laughed and nodded towards David. 'He doesn't, that's for sure.'

'Come on, Kenny, neither do you!'

'But why?' Veronica pressed. 'It's just a graveyard, after all.'

David shook his head. 'When I was a lad, an old ghillie told me he'd been on the island and seen ghostly figures there; others have too, down the years. I *have* been on there, a long time ago, but it felt too spooky, so I just leave the place alone these days.'

Kenny nodded. 'There's certainly an atmosphere out there. I have to admit to not liking the place very much myself.'

'You're not alone, Kenny,' John grunted. 'The ruddy sea trout don't seem that keen, either!'

SILHOUETTE IN THE RIVER

Sea trout fishing at night is incredibly exciting, but it can be weird as well. Nocturnal noises can be put down to local wildlife and visions in the darkness logically explained away in the cold light of day. Or can they?

David was a highly experienced fisherman with a particular love for sea trout. He travelled far for his fishing, at home as much on the lochs and loughs of western Scotland and Ireland as he was on the rivers of south west Wales and England. The identity of the river he was fishing on this particular night is not known, nor are the real names of the pools in question. David didn't want to draw attention to the actual venue so he has kept the details secret. Oh, and his real name isn't David, either.

The session began quite normally. Dinner in the hotel had been excellent and he had kept his alcohol intake down to a glass of wine with his meal and a small nip of whisky with his coffee, a ritual he always followed before venturing out to hunt sea trout. Dusk was drawing in as he walked down to the river, there was good cloud cover and it was warm without being muggy. The portents for a decent night's fishing were excellent.

David waited until the light was practically gone from the western sky before he waded out into the neck of the Stream, a beautiful piece of fly water that fished well for salmon by day and held good sea trout numbers at this time of year. He knew, having spoken earlier to the keeper, that no one had been on the river that afternoon, so the pool should be rested and the fish undisturbed. He couldn't ask for anything much better as he cast a small black tube fly across the river on a sink tip line. There were some big, early season fish about and he was confident he would connect with one before the night was out.

The first session, as he always called the period up to midnight, was uneventful, and he came ashore to have a cup of coffee from his flask and another nip of whisky, just enough to put a warm glow into his stomach and keep out the chill of the river water. He had listened to three types of owl so far: a screeching barn, a tawny and an impish little owl, which kept perching on a nearby fence post and letting everyone know he was around with his shrill call. David was well used to all this, though, as he was to the regular bark of a dog fox somewhere over in the wood, and it only added to the atmosphere as far as he was concerned.

He went back into the water at about 12.30, having changed to a full sunk line and a bigger black fly. There was slightly less cloud now, so that a little light shone through occasionally from the moon, enough to pick out trees and bankside rocks in silhouette. His plan was to fish down the Stream again, then wade into the neck of the next pool, known as the Meadow. He had kept that until this second session because the keeper had said the Meadow was his best chance of a really big sea trout at this time of year, although it usually fished better after midnight.

He made his way slowly down until he reached the slower flow at the bottom of the pool, where he added extra movement to the fly with a figure-of-eight retrieve. At one point he looked away from the inky water in front of him, downstream to the Meadow, and was shocked to see that there was another angler fishing there. The person was standing at the neck of the pool, the silhouette of his top half against the sky and the rest of him less distinct against the water. He was in exactly the spot David was planning to be in a few moments, which was frustrating, because the keeper had told him he would be the only one out there tonight. It was also strange that the other fisher, whoever he or she was, hadn't bothered to come up and make contact, which was the etiquette on this particular beat so that they could agree where each would fish. The obvious explanation was that the figure was a poacher!

David's attention was grabbed back to his own pool as his rod was suddenly pulled down by a hard tug, and he was into a good sea trout that immediately came out of the water and went back with a loud *smack*! As line came off the reel and the ratchet sounded impressively loud in the night air, David glanced back at the Meadow and expected to see the figure beating a hasty retreat from the river. The poacher must have heard the splash and then the reel, which would surely frighten him away from his illegal activities. Instead, though, the silhouette was still there, motionless, and David had the distinct impression that the figure was watching him. He felt slightly peculiar and unnerved; an alien situation for him.

He played the sea trout for some while. It was a bigger fish than he had first thought, probably in the 5- to 7-pound class, he decided. But he couldn't really concentrate on the fight, because he found himself continually glancing over his left shoulder to see whether the figure was still there. The longer the tussle went on, the more he thought the figure might come up and help him, as it must be obvious he was into a decent fish.

The silhouette remained unmoved and David was just about to call out when the rod sprang back and the fish was gone.

'Bugger!' he shouted. 'That was a bloody good fish.'

No reaction from the figure whatsoever. No movement, no *bad luck* response, or *what fly were you using*? It just stood there and David began to feel seriously unnerved. If he stayed on the river, would the poacher, determined to catch some fish for himself, come over and attack him? David was a visitor to the region, after all, and some of the locals probably considered that the water was morally theirs after dark, no matter who reckoned they owned the fishing rights.

'Well, it's getting late, so I think I'll leave you to it,' he called out as loudly as he could. 'There's always tomorrow!'

He waded ashore, walked swiftly up the bank to collect his bag and then was off along the path to the hotel as fast as his legs would carry him. He had never felt like this before, not since his earliest days of being on the river after dark. The adrenalin was rushing through his body and he couldn't wait to get back to his room and attack the whisky bottle.

'How did you get on last night?' asked the keeper when David joined him in the hotel's rod room in the morning.

'Hooked one and lost it,' said David. 'Tell me, do you have any poaching problems round here?'

The keeper shook his head. 'Nothing to speak of. Why?'

David told him what had happened and the keeper listened increasingly intently.

'You're sure it was a human figure?'

'Yes, I am. Anyway, what else could it have been, standing in the middle of the river like that?

'A cow or a deer or something?'

'I don't think so, it was definitely a man.'

'Yes, I was afraid you'd say that.'

'Are you alright?' David asked, as the man's face had gone pale. 'Look, what's all this about?'

The keeper shrugged and sat down. 'Um. . . there's no easy way to say this. I think you probably saw a ghost on the river last night.'

A heavy weight sank into David's guts. 'A ghost? Whose flipping ghost?'

'If it's who I think it was, he was a guy called Herbert Tattershall, who used to fish this beat for sea trout years ago.'

David stared at him. 'So how did he die?'

'He drowned. It had been raining up in the headwaters, apparently, but not down this far, so the theory was that the river came up without him really noticing it in the dark. When he stepped off the bank into the neck of the Meadow to start fishing, he was swept away. He was nearly 70, so he just wasn't strong enough to fight his way out.'

David breathed out. 'Bloody hell,' he said quietly, feeling the hairs on the back of his neck and hands start to prickle. His body shook involuntarily at the memory of that silhouetted figure glaring through the darkness at him.

The keeper was quiet for a moment or two, then looked at David with an embarrassed expression. 'This has happened a few times before and always under the same conditions. You probably haven't seen the river this morning, but it's come up a hell of a lot since you were out there fishing; it's been raining up on the moor, just like it did when Herbert Tattershall drowned.'

'Okay, so why was he haunting my fishing last night?'

'Well, if my theory's right, he was trying to scare you off the river, just like he was with the others when he appeared before. I think he was trying to make sure none of you met the same fate as he did.'

PART FOUR

Amazing Days

ORKNEY OLIVES AND
SEA TROUT

Fishing tales don't necessarily need massive fish to make them stand out in the memory. They can stem from ordinary days that were spent seeking nothing more than the chance of a few fish and some solitude, especially if nature intervenes.

Every year, I used to go to Orkney, off the north coast of Scotland. In fact, I think I went for 12 consecutive years, fishing with the same ghillie, Geordie Leonard, each time. I even ended up being Geordie's best man at his wedding, giving a speech to the assembled company in Stromness on the day England beat Scotland in the European Cup, thanks to a wonder goal from Paul Gasgoine. That was a particularly daunting job for a Sassenach to carry out, but as I had caught my first ever Orkney 2-pound trout that morning, fishing at dawn with Geordie on Swannay Loch, I wasn't too concerned. And I needn't have worried anyway; the Orcadians are far too decent to hold being an Englishman against anyone for very long.

Harray is the main freshwater loch on the Orkney Islands. It runs into the brackish Loch of Stenness, memorable not only for its fishing but for the ancient standing stones on its shore. The trout fishing on Harray is legendary: buttery brown and brightly spotted fish which fight incredibly hard for their size taking the fly in the shallow water around the shores and myriad skerries throughout the loch. In the pan for breakfast, they are some of the best-tasting fish I have eaten anywhere in the world.

This day on Harray started much like countless others. Geordie picked up my fishing colleague, Peter, and me in his heavy fibreglass boat, which I have to say my back problems of the time helped to design. Few people now go afloat without smart factory-made boat seats, but in those days they were little more than a thwart board across the gunwales to get you a bit higher and make casting easier. My back was such that sitting in a boat for an extended period became agony, so a couple of years before, Geordie had produced an old kitchen chair for me to put on the floor in the stern, which was a brilliant success. The only interesting moments came during long Harray swells, when the boat's broadside motion would sometimes tip the chair to a dangerous angle, although I never actually ended up over the side. Geordie had been hard at work over the winter and the boat now boasted fixed bow and stern swivel seats, which made fishing a delight in any weather, and us the envy of everyone else on the loch.

We started catching brownies in front of the Merkister Hotel, Geordie quietly edging the boat out into the main body of the loch as we did. Then something huge swirled some 30 yards in front of us, not at anyone's fly, just completely out of the blue.

'Salmon!' shouted Geordie. 'You don't see many of those in here.'

Then it swirled again and we saw it more clearly this time. 'Looks a bit coloured,' I said.

'Positively brown,' agreed Peter.

'And furry,' Geordie added. 'That's a flaming otter!'

And so we watched the otter fishing for a few more moments until it finally caught a brown trout, considerably bigger than anything we had brought to the boat that week. The animal ate it quickly on the surface and dived back under. We didn't see it again, as hard as we looked for it all around the boat. Unbelievable as it seemed in that expanse of water, the otter simply disappeared.

We caught plenty more fish during the morning and decided to go back to the Merkister for lunch, rather than our normal habit of landing on one of the many islands in the loch. There were plenty of people in the bar to hear Geordie's account of the morning, but it was soon obvious that no one believed a word of it.

'I've lived on this loch all my life,' said an octogenarian Orcadian from his favourite chair by the window overlooking the water, 'and I've never seen an otter. They're there, I have no doubt, but you never see them, especially in broad daylight.'

He was supported by everyone else, including the Merkister's proprietor from behind the bar, who professed that he had been at the hotel for donkeys' years and had never set eyes on an otter either. And so we endured the good-natured banter and suggestions that the sloe gin must have been liberally passed round the boat early that morning. We finished our lunch and went afloat again.

We usually caught the odd sea trout in the loch, but we often had to look very carefully to spot the difference from the freshwater variety, as they were usually coloured by the time they made it through Stenness into Harray. This afternoon, we started a drift from Cutlass Point right across the main body of the loch's northern end and all of a sudden olives began to hatch. The air was full of them, as often in those days, and fish were moving to them, breaking the surface in a feeding frenzy. We started catching them on Greenwell's Glories, that old favourite invented for just a moment such as that. But the fish weren't coloured, they were all bars of silver between 12 ounces and $1^3/_4$ pounds. We were experiencing yet another first for us on Harray: a shoal of fresh-run sea trout that must have made it through Stenness in record time and swum just as quickly to this end of the loch.

The magic went on for perhaps an hour, with Geordie bringing us back for drift after drift over the same ground.

'Just once more,' he said each time. 'They won't still be there, but we've got to give them another go.'

They were still there, though, gorging on the olives, so don't let anyone tell you sea trout won't feed in fresh water. These ones were doing so as though their very existence depended on it.

It was probably our fifth drift over the same ground when Geordie spoke about something other than olives and sea trout, and how he had never seen anything like this in more than 10 years as a ghillie.

'Strange, that skerry's high out of the water,' he said.

Skerries are small outcrops of rock that poke above the surface of the loch, often as tiny stony beaches in the middle of otherwise seemingly deep water. Despite being 3000 acres in area, Harray is seldom more than 6 feet deep and these shallow areas were always the best for fishing back then. This one seemed peculiar, though. Geordie was right: it was too high out of the water.

We were about 100 yards away when the stones started to move, then slid off the back of the skerry.

'I do not believe it,' shouted Peter. 'It's a *seal*!'

'No,' said Geordie, 'your perspective's all wrong. It was that otter again.'

Then the most remarkable thing happened. No more than 20 yards in front of us, the otter came up just like a seal, bobbing in the water and looking straight at us, as though it had never seen humans before and it was fascinated by what we were doing there.

'It's huge,' I said. 'No way is that the same animal we saw this morning.'

'It's a dog otter,' Geordie agreed. 'Definitely different from this morning.'

The otter kept watching us, although we never seemed to get any closer, despite the fact we were drifting. He must have been backpedalling to keep his distance while he studied these strange people invading his watery habitat, and then, like the earlier encounter, he simply slipped below the surface and was gone.

'I'm going to enjoy hearing you describe this one in the bar tonight,' I told Geordie. 'It might be better to keep quiet about it, because no bugger's going to believe us.'

They didn't, of course, and still don't to this day, I'm sure, even though they were all pretty impressed with the bag of sea trout, which must have signalled to them that something out of the ordinary had happened on Harray that day. I've discussed it with Geordie many times since and the conclusion we've come to is that the otters were probably sea dwellers, and had followed, or even frightened, the sea trout into Harray. This may also account for the feeding frenzy, perhaps because the fish would normally have stayed to feed longer in the brackish Stenness before coming into Harray, although that probably hasn't much foundation in proven fisheries science.

Whatever the reason, it was one of the most remarkable day's fishing I have ever had the privilege to experience, and it taught me, if I needed teaching, that catching monsters isn't the only ingredient necessary to enjoy this fantastic sport of ours.

STORM-TOSSED SALMON

Even in the most unpromising situations, it is often better just to trust the professionals and go with the flow; sometimes literally. Very occasionally, this results in the fishing session of a lifetime.

Salmon anglers have a seemingly bottomless pit of excuses as to why they can't catch fish. It's either too hot or too cold, the barometric pressure is too high or falling too quickly, it's raining too hard or there hasn't been any rain at all recently, or there simply aren't enough fish in the river or lough. And many experienced fishermen will take one look at the weather in the morning and dismiss any chance of taking a fish that day, for any one of myriad reasons.

Ghillies can be just as bad. For instance, many of them slavishly abide by the old myth that if the morning mist is down over the hills, salmon fishing will be futile. The wind is rarely from the right direction, the river is too high or showing its bones, or the tide out in the bay is all wrong to throw any fresh fish into the river that day. Defeatism can be in the air before a line has been cast, and there are those who say this attitude is transmitted down the line to the fish, which is the ultimate excuse for failing to attract even a sniff of a salmon.

The scene was thus set at the breakfast table in the marvellous Delphi Lodge in Ireland's County Mayo, on the edge of Connemara. George and his wife, Helen, were drinking coffee and eyeing up the branches of the pine trees being swept around in a ferocious wind, and the rain sheeting horizontally against the windows, as it had been since midnight. They were wondering why they had ever bothered getting out of bed so early on such an obviously lousy day for fishing. The idea of venturing forth in the forlorn hope of catching a salmon in those conditions seemed outrageous.

'We're supposed to be on the lough this morning,' said George, 'and Peter will be waiting for us.'

'What, just to say *don't bother?*'

'Come on, at least we can show willing. I'd prefer him to call it off rather than us, then we can decide what to do with the rest of the day.'

They donned jackets, over-trousers, caps and hoods, and walked down to the landing stage at the edge of Finlough. Peter was waiting for them, dressed as though he was about to attempt a walk to the North Pole, and the only thing out of place with the whole scenario was the wide grin across their ghillie's face.

'Morning. Ready to go fishing, then?'

'Peter, you're joking, aren't you? I wouldn't walk down the riverbank, let alone go out in a boat on the lough in this lot.'

'Well now, I've fished here all my life and I've not lost an angler yet. I dare say I'll not be starting with either of you two today.'

Helen winced. 'But the wind, Peter, and the rain? Surely no self-respecting salmon's going to take in these conditions.'

The grin widened. 'You'll wait your whole life for a day like this on the salmon. Trust me. The wind's veering into the south and that alone means it'll be worth a cast or two. Come on now, you're both experienced enough to fish in this, otherwise I wouldn't suggest it. It's just a question of confidence.'

George shuffled his feet, not sure what to do. The whole idea seemed preposterous, and he was completely thrown by Peter's enthusiasm.

He'd always been a great ghillie for them and was the first to voice his opinions when the chances were zilch. George was convinced they were less than zilch right now, so what was going on?

'Okay, Peter, we'll go and fetch the gear, but we'll only stay out for an hour. I'm not contracting pneumonia on a wild salmon chase.'

'And I'll be reminding you about that statement in an hour or so,' said Peter, a twinkle in his eye and the grin as wide as it was possible to go. 'So 12-pound casts, please, and only two flies out there today. Something black and flashy on the point, like a silver stoat, and your usual muddler on the bob. Quickly, now.'

Tackling up took time, mainly due to the wind continually catching the nylon and cold, wet fingers refusing to function as normal. Finally, though, they were in the boat and, hands thrust deep into pockets and backs to the bow, they set out from the landing stage. Once clear of the headland, the bows dug deep into the waves and sent water cascading into the boat, straight over George and Helen, who were sitting hunched up and trying desperately to stop any leakage down their necks. Thankfully, the trip didn't last long and soon they were up at the top reed-bed. Peter positioned the boat, then cut the engine and went onto the oars, with George in the stern seat and Helen up in the bows.

The first thing George noticed was that Peter's local forecast had turned out to be accurate: the wind had, indeed, swung from a cold easterly into the warmer south. Even so, the surrounding hills funnel the wind down the Delphi and swirl it round Finlough, making boat handling and casting very difficult in stormy weather. Peter was a past master at holding the boat's drift, but George's first cast was intercepted by a sudden cross-wind and collapsed in a spaghetti heap a few yards in front of him. He muttered under his breath a heartfelt *what the hell are we doing out here?*

'Short lines, George,' Peter suggested. 'The salmon won't worry how close they come to the boat in this wave.'

George grunted, sorted out his line and cast again, this time just long enough for him to work the muddler through the surface. His concentration was fixed firmly on the wake of the fly across the water, when a mouth suddenly appeared and slashed violently at it. There was a tug, but then nothing.

'Damn, that was a fish!' he cried out in stunned surprise.

Peter laughed. 'I told you. . .'

'I've got one!' shouted Helen from the bow, and George glanced over to see his wife's single-handed rod bouncing around as she played an energetic salmon adroitly in the heavy wave. She finally brought the fish in behind the boat and Peter leant over the gunwale to net a bright silver grilse of about 5 pounds, sea lice still attached to its tail wrist.

'That was swimming around the bay this morning,' said Peter. 'You couldn't ask for a fresher salmon off the tide than that.'

No sooner had Helen's grilse hit the deck boards than George had another fish swirl at the muddler, then the rod tip was pulled down sharply as the salmon turned and hit the silver stoat on the point. Even as he played the fish, three or four grilse head and tailed in the vicinity of the boat, and George had the distinct impression that they were floating in salmon soup.

Although Peter had expertly slowed the speed of the boat's drift, they were bearing quickly down the stream that leads into the middle river, in which the salmon lie when they first come up into the lough. Almost every cast resulted in a swirl at the muddler or a pull on the point, much more like trout than salmon fishing, and then both George and Helen were into fish and playing them at the same time. Even Peter now, with all his years of experience at ghillieing, was getting genuinely excited, trying to control the boat and net two grilse at the same time.

Once those two were in the boat, Peter started the engine and motored back towards the top of the drift again. 'We've been out from the dock about an hour,' he shouted above the noise of the engine. 'I take it we'll be heading back now?'

George kept a straight face. 'Well, perhaps just another 10 minutes.'

Peter laughed and pointed a finger. 'Told you so!'

After three hours' fishing, they had landed 10 salmon, hooked and lost a further half dozen and had countless swirls and pulls at the flies, as well as seeing well over 100 fish show on the surface up and down the lough. If it had been a trout-fishing session it would have been spectacular enough, but the fact that they were all salmon made it some of the most remarkable fishing ever experienced on the Delphi system.

Back on land again, with the rain still hammering down, George shook Peter by the hand. 'How did you know that was going to happen?'

Peter tapped his nose with his finger. 'I've known three, maybe four days like this in 40 years on the Delphi. The barometer's low, which means the fish shouldn't take at all, but it's that combination of a big spring tide throwing a huge run of fresh salmon into the system coinciding with a complete change of wind from cold to warm that did it. And they'll not take like that this afternoon, you know? You've had the best of it, and you'll probably never have fishing like that in your life again.'

'But how did you know the fish would run today?'

'Because I was out in the bay last evening, looking to see whether the mackerel were in yet, and I saw the shoal of salmon there, waiting for the tide. I heard the rain in the night and I knew they'd be straight through the lower river and into the lough this morning, and then we'd have just a few hours before they settled into their lies. Believe me, George, very few people ever get to experience fishing like that.'

George grinned. 'And there was me thinking it was just down to our skill at fishing a muddler!'

AUSTRALIAN MARLIN
AND SASHIMI

A polite enquiry, a stroke of luck and a clear head lead to an unforgettable day's fishing.

Mark was looking for a break on a long business trip in northern Australia. Having spent a fortnight in the bush advising on management options for some wetland areas, he was now in Cairns, generally considered to be the marlin capital of the world. He went down to the harbour as the sport fishing boats came home, waited for the clients to disembark and hailed one of the skippers.

'Any chance of a trip in the next couple of days?'

'No, mate, fully booked. So's everyone else at the moment: fishing's brilliant out there and every bugger wants a slice of the action.'

'No chance at all?' he pleaded.

The skipper took off his baseball hat and scratched his head. 'You do a lot of fishing, do you?'

'Yes, all over the world.'

The skipper nodded. 'Okay, come out with my party tomorrow. They're a group of Japanese businessmen and I don't think they've much idea what they're doing. My crewman's got a doctor's appointment, so if you help me get these guys some fish, I'll see if we can put you on the end of something before the day's out and I won't charge you anything. How's that?'

'Great. What time?'

Mark spent the night in one of the smarter hotels, paid for under his consultancy fee. In the bar after dinner, he happened to notice a group of well-dressed Japanese. They were obviously hell-bent on enjoying themselves, as the whisky was flowing freely and there wasn't much of a gap between rounds. They couldn't be the fishing party, though, not the way they were drinking, and that was confirmed later when they transferred en masse into the all-night casino, just before Mark went up to bed.

He arrived in good time and helped the skipper, Don, prepare the tackle for the Japanese. Departure hour arrived, but no fishing party. While all the other boats were leaving harbour full of anglers, Don and Mark could only drink coffee and wait.

'These business groups have a bit of a reputation round here,' said Don. 'Plenty of fire water, gambling and the odd lady of the night before they come fishing. From my experience, don't expect too much from them today!'

The Japanese party finally arrived 45 minutes behind schedule, and was indeed the same group from the previous evening. From the look of their condition, they were regretting the fact that they had booked a fishing trip after such a heavy night. They certainly didn't look prepared for tackling an apex predator out in the open ocean.

Mark cast off the mooring lines and Don nosed the boat out of the harbour. Once at sea, they were met with a heavy swell and, to a man, the Japanese went into shutdown mode, either in the wheelhouse or just lying down on the deck with backs against the gunwales. It wasn't a great omen for a successful day's fishing.

Don steamed for a short while, watching the echo sounder until he reached a rough piece of ground. He then slowed the boat so that Mark could pay out the trolling lures, the idea being that he would hook a fish and then call one of the Japanese over to play it. Almost immediately, the first lure was hit by a small express train and he struck into something that dived deep and doggedly stayed there.

Mark looked behind him, expecting to see a line of excited Japanese vying to be the first one to land a fish. However, all those on deck had their eyes closed and no one seemed in a hurry to leave the wheelhouse.

'Bring it in yourself,' Don called out.

'Oh, okay.'

Mark leant into the fish and tried to power it to the surface, but it wasn't quite that easy. Each time he had it close to the top it bored away again, and it was a good six or seven minutes before he had it under control beside the boat.

Don flew out of the wheelhouse, leant over and hauled the fish inboard. 'This isn't going to be easy without a crew. Can you handle it yourself?'

'Yeah, no problem. What is it?'

'King mackerel, about 15 pounds.'

The next fish did the exact opposite to the first, spending a good deal of its time in the air.

'Any takers?' Mark shouted over his shoulder.

'They're all asleep,' Don shouted. 'Just keep 'em coming and enjoy yourself!'

The sport became frenetic. That second fish was a wahoo, and it was followed by jacks, two yellow-fin tuna, a mahimahi, more king mackerel and a decent-sized giant trevally. A tuna slapped around the deck and made enough noise to rouse one of the fishing party out of his stupor, and he was galvanised into enough action to take the rod and play a lively Queenfish, which meant that Don could stay on the wheel while Mark played crew and boated the fish. However, although the Japanese seemed delighted and extremely grateful for the opportunity of some sport, he went straight back to his berth and was soon unconscious again.

Mark poked his head into the wheelhouse. 'I feel a bit of a fraud, taking all the fishing like this.'

'Don't! The trip's all paid for, so it's up to them whether they want to take part or sleep. Look, we've got some bait now; d'you fancy a go at a proper sport fish?'

Mark was having huge fun where they were, but he knew the whole point of this trip, and the reason the Japanese had spent so much money on it, was to try to catch a black marlin.

He grinned. 'It'd be rude not to, wouldn't it?'

The swell increased as they went out further, the boat crashing uncomfortably through the lumpy seas. This prompted one of the Japanese to wake up rather quickly and be violently ill over the side. He crawled back into the wheelhouse, in no condition to tackle the bait let alone a marlin.

Once they reached the main fishing grounds, Don came out and showed Mark how to hook up a jack as bait. He paid it out astern of the boat on the big game tackle, then left Mark in charge of the deck while he went back into the wheelhouse and began the troll.

For Mark the suspense was electric, knowing that this was as a good a place as anywhere on the planet to connect with a big marlin. Don had told him over coffee that morning that his boat had already landed more than 20 granders, marlin of 1000 pounds or more in weight, with the biggest just over 1100 pounds. He had no perception of what playing a fish of that size would be like, although he had plenty of time to think about it as they trolled the baits through the swell.

After a good few hours, the ratchet on one of the massive multiplier reels suddenly started screaming. Mark engaged the clutch and struck into the fish, which went solid for a second or two then roared away, stripping line off the extremely expensive-looking multiplier's spool against what he assumed was a state-of-the-art braking system. By the speed it was moving, the marlin obviously wasn't very impressed.

'Harness up, Mark!' Don yelled, then ran onto deck and helped him into the fighting chair. 'Sorry, mate, but you're on your own with this one. I've got to stay on the wheel. Will you be okay?'

'What about our Japanese friends, isn't there one. . .?'

'Just stay put. I want this fish, okay?'

That was the cue for the marlin to break through the surface, its long bill pointed skywards as it cut through a trough between the swells and disappeared into the next wall of water before boring away into the depths. The adrenalin was pumping through Mark's body now, with the exhilaration of seeing the fish so early in the fight. The power surging up the line was unbelievable.

The fight lasted about 80 minutes of searing runs, tail-walks, deep-boring dives and heart-stopping head shakes. Just about everything a fish could do to try to escape, that one did. It wasn't so much sport as arm-wrestling with primordial powers, and Mark wondered who would break first. Eventually, though, he sensed the marlin tire, and he was gradually able to coax it to the surface with the enormous power available from the big game rod and reel, and then to the side of the boat.

Don put the engines into neutral and came out on deck wearing thick gloves.

'Brilliant, mate! Hold him steady while I. . .'

He leant over the side and clasped the marlin round the base of the bill with one hand and the wire trace with the other.

'. . .try to control this bugger. Can you unhitch yourself and give me a hand here?'

Mark climbed out of the fighting chair and took hold of the marlin's bill, which enabled Don to use both hands to work the hook free.

'Got a camera?'

'Not with me. . .'

'No problem, I take pictures,' said a heavily accented voice from behind. Mark looked back over his shoulder to see a grinning Japanese taking photographs.

'Okay, that's enough,' Don said. 'Let her go back now.'

The fish stayed beside the boat looking at them for a few moments, then sank down, twisted away and disappeared.

The Japanese shook Mark's hand vigorously. 'Very good. We catch huge fish, yes?'

Mark made all the right noises about wishing one of the party had caught the marlin, but the Japanese seemed genuinely delighted that *someone* had caught a fish. Meanwhile, Don had opened up the boat's big diesels and they were powering back through the swell towards Cairns.

Mark tidied the tackle and joined him in the wheelhouse. 'How big was the marlin?'

'About 450, 475, something like that. Not a grander, but a bloody good fish, just the same. Not bad, considering you haven't paid a cent for the trip!'

Once they reached calmer water, Don motioned for Mark to take the wheel.

'I know what'll cheer this lot up. Just keep heading straight as you go.' He then went out on deck and made for the cold box at the stern.

The Japanese were all awake now and talking excitedly about the marlin, looking at the pictures on the camera and seemingly as happy as though they had caught the fish themselves. They were even happier when Don came back into the wheelhouse a while later, carrying a wooden board covered in thin strips of raw fish, with a bottle of soy sauce and a tube of wasabi paste. He was clearly experienced at dealing with this sort of clientele.

'You guys deserve something out of this trip. Here, try this sushi stuff for size. That's best Aussie yellow-fin tuna, that is, and it's been on ice since this morning. Go on, tuck in!'

Mark took the tiniest piece himself, just to show willing, but the Japanese wolfed down the rest as though their lives depended on it; so much so that Don cut up another fillet's worth for them. Mark grinned at their enthusiasm, not to mention their resilience, as he settled back into the helmsman's chair.

He couldn't believe his luck at such a fantastic day's sport and decided it was time to say a silent thank-you for the delayed effects of Scottish whisky, gambling dens and whatever else this lot did at night when their wives weren't around.

COLONIAL FLASHBACK

The Indian Ocean has long been a big-game fisher's paradise, one of the great adventures for the global angler. But the world has changed from Kenya's colonial past and conservation has a stronger pull on the modern angler.

I n 1998 Peter Spillett, his partner Yvette and children Rebecca and James, had enjoyed a two-week Kenyan safari and were based near Malindi on the east African coast for a few days' relaxation before going home to the UK. He had always been a bit ambivalent about big-game fishing: concern about the destruction of apex predators such as billfish pitted against the thrill of seeing and catching such large, exciting species. The family had already noticed the bleaching of coral caused by pollution and warming sea temperatures, while snorkelling over the reef of the local lagoon, and didn't want to contribute to any further degradation of the marine ecology.

However, the opportunity to go fishing beyond the reef finally won the struggle, and Peter and James joined a boat heading out of Malindi with a skipper and three crewmen. The other guests were a married couple, although the side effects of malaria tablets kept the wife lying in the wheelhouse, quietly moaning, for the entire trip, so there were only three anglers to share whatever spoils the Indian Ocean had to offer.

Just beyond the reef, they had great fun for half an hour catching small bonito. Knowing that James was an ardent conservationist who was against unnecessary killing, Peter was relieved to see all the fish going alive into a tank, although he wasn't quite sure why. The boat then headed further out to sea and, with an increasing swell making the going bumpy, they soon spied a flock of skuas, terns and gulls diving into some turbulent water up ahead.

'Baitfish!' stated the skipper. 'There are predators underneath pushing them up on the surface. Just what we want.'

The fate of the bonito now became clear. They were whipped out of the tank, their flanks were slit with a knife and they were impaled and tied to a big-game hook and cast over the side. The whole process was rather gory and the deck was splattered with blood, in stark contrast to James's face, which, after witnessing that operation, seemed distinctly paler under the tan he had gained in the bush.

James was the first to get a strike when a magnificent sailfish shot out of the water and tail-walked across the surface, iridescent colours bursting from its huge dorsal fin in the sunlight. Everyone became very excited and the crewmen hovered behind James, giving him equal measures of advice and encouragement as he battled the fish. He handled it really well, but was exhausted by the time he finally brought the fish alongside after a 20-minute fight.

Peter was just about to say something about releasing the fish when one of the crewmen leant over the side and clubbed the sailfish to death with a weighted wooden cosh. He and a colleague sank gaffs into its flanks and hauled it aboard. Catch and release didn't seem to be first priority with the crew, so Peter bit his tongue on the subject, despite James's obvious disappointment that his quarry had had to die.

'Nice fish,' shouted the skipper from the wheelhouse. 'About 60, 70 pounds.'

The other guest was next to take a fish, a carbon copy of James's sailfish and one that met a similar fate. It was then Peter's turn to be strapped into the fighting chair and it wasn't long before something big hit his bonito bait. He leant back into the fish and waited for another spectacular tail-walk across the surface, but that didn't happen this time. Instead, the fish stayed deep, feeling very heavy and powerful.

'Could it be a marlin?' he asked.

'Might be,' said one of the crew. 'Big fish, anyway.'

Peter fought a battle of attrition with the fish for more than half an hour, gaining line painfully slowly against what was, for the most part, a dead weight on the other end. At times it was like playing a log of wood, except that the occasional head shake and short, dogged run proved that he was hooked up to something animate.

The wire trace finally emerged from the water and a long, grey-brown shape slowly materialised from the depths.

'Shark, shark!' a crewman shouted at the skipper, and they all became very agitated.

Peter managed to bring the fish close in to the port side, whereupon all three crewmen leant over and clubbed the shark relentlessly until it stopped thrashing. It was hauled unceremoniously over the gunwale onto the deck, where the Africans kept their distance from the fish until they were sure it was dead.

'Spinner,' the skipper identified the shark from the wheelhouse door. 'Nice fish. I reckon 150. Good catch.'

One of the crewman plucked up the courage to go forward and extract the hook from the shark's mouth. He was obviously no fan of sharks and looked genuinely scared of this one, despite the number of times it had been smacked over the head. Now, though, just at the critical moment when the hook was about to come loose, the fish gave an energetically nervous shake of its head. The hook, under tension from the line being held tightly, flew out and lodged firmly in the back of the crew's hand.

After an initial yelp, he seemed quite calm about the accident, even when the skipper tried unsuccessfully to pull it out.

'Nah, that's a doctor job,' said the skipper. 'It's time we went home anyway.'

The skipper opened up the boat's two powerful diesel engines, leaving the crewmen to deal with the catch. Rope nooses were tied round the tail wrist of all three fish, which were hauled over and tied to the transom in a neat line. As they headed back to the now distant shore, nursing a very welcome cold beer, it was rather poignant to see the once vivid colours on the sailfishes' dorsal fins gradually fade into dullness.

As they neared land, the crewman hoisted flags up to the masthead.

'It shows what we've caught,' said the skipper. The grin across his face suggested Peter's suspicions were probably justified: the dead fish arranged across the stern were there as a great advertisement for his boat as they entered harbour, designed to procure more bookings from any fishing tourists who might be around when they landed.

And then, as the boat entered Malindi harbour – and for several hours afterwards for that matter – they went into a time warp, as though they had been transported back to the east African colonial era, when this sort of thing would have been the norm. The skipper had obviously used his radio to report his catch well in advance of reaching port, and the quay was crowded with people, both locals and tourists. They swarmed round and there was much excited chatter as the fish were brought ashore and hauled up on the scales, tail first, to be weighed. As expected, the sailfish were both around 60 pounds and the spinner shark 155.

Once weighed, the fish were lowered to the ground and the skipper and crewmen, including the one with the hook still in his hand, were helped by some of the locals to cut the fish into manageable pieces.

'What are they doing that for?' asked Peter. 'I thought you'd sell them.'

'Nah, they'll go to the old folk and the poor who can't afford to buy fish.'

'Oh, right.' That made him feel a good deal better about the killing bit. 'What, even the shark?'

'Especially the shark. People love them round here.'

The wounded crewman wandered off to find the doctor while the skipper took Peter and James, now reunited with Yvette and Rebecca, into the fishing clubhouse on the waterfront. This was colonial elegance in all its prewar splendour, freshly painted walls covered in fishing trophies, fans slowly revolving from the ceiling and waiters in white coats and gloves serving drinks. It was a complete throwback.

The beer was ice cold as well. Peter was just relishing his when he realised that there was the cast of an enormous billfish at the far end of the lounge, its flank all silver and hazy blue.

'What the hell's that?'

'Indo-Pacific blue marlin,' replied the skipper. 'Kenyan record for a while. It weighed 1500 pounds and towed us around the Indian Ocean for 14 hours. The only way we killed it in the end was to haul it backwards so we drowned it. Biggest fish I've ever had in the boat.'

Just before they left, Peter wandered into the next room and was confronted by the alarming sight of an outlandishly huge shark's head. 'And what about *that*, for God's sake. Did you catch that as well?'

'Nah, not that one. It's a great white, weighed nearly a tonne.'

'I guess it was caught well out to sea?'

'Nah, no way. It was tangled up in fishermen's nets at the entrance to the lagoon.'

Peter stared at him and there was stunned silence for a few seconds. 'You're joking, aren't you?'

'Straight up.'

'But we were snorkelling round there yesterday. Loads of other people were too.'

'Yeah, I'm sure.'

Suffice to say that Peter's family stuck firmly to the hotel's swimming pool for the rest of their stay.

GREEDY AUSTRALIAN TROUT

The eternal question of whether or not fish feel pain when hooked and played on a rod and line will probably never be answered satisfactorily until humans learn to converse with aquatic life. Or will it?

Many biologists suggest that fish do not have the required sensory system to feel as humans do, especially in mouths that have no nerves. However, others use elaborate tests, such as injecting bee venom into a laboratory rainbow trout and observing the odd twitch down its body, as proof positive that the fish must be in agony when hooked.

Non-scientific anglers will point to the more common-sense approach: if fish really do feel pain as higher mammals do, would they eat snails, crayfish and spiny-finned prey fish, or fight so hard against the

126

pressure of the angler's rod? Wouldn't they just surrender meekly, rather than run off into the distance against the tightened clutch of a modern reel? And anyway, what about the trout from Hampshire's River Avon that was seen to be jumping out of the water at a swarm of bees and, when finally caught on a hastily tied bee imitation, killed and gutted, was absolutely stuffed full of the insects, some of whom must have used their stings in a vain attempt to evade capture?

An incident happened in southern Australia that might shed some light on this thorny issue. As with many non-scientific experiments, the results were inconclusive, but certainly gave those involved an amazing experience that they believe to this day to be unique. However, before telling the story, it is important to know something of the history and landscape behind the action that day.

Brown trout fishing in Tasmania, the island off the southernmost shore of Australia, really took off when the government constructed several dams in the Western Highlands to produce hydro-powered electricity for the state. The flooding water covered fertile land that produced food aplenty for the brown trout, which were first introduced into Tasmania from England more than a century before. They grow at incredible speed and, in Arthur's Lake, sunken trees, remnants of a flooded forest, still stand and provide a great habitat for marauding fish. Better still, the surrounding gum trees produce an endless supply of terrestrial bugs, clouds of psylla and beetles, which are blown onto the lakes and provide valuable protein for the foraging fish. The wind lanes on these waters corral the insects and provide a highway for trout to cruise upwind, picking off food particles at will until they are utterly gorged.

This was the scene when Dr Brett Wolf, a fly-fishing aficionado who used to run Blue Lake Lodge, took George and Helen Westropp on their first trip on Arthur's Lake. The wind was blowing steadily from the south and creating wide wind lanes close to shore, right above the desiccated tree trunks; it was immediately obvious that the trout were feeding in them on the terrestrial bugs.

'What flies, Brett?' asked George.

'Anything you like . . . just so long as it's the Para Dun!'

'Don't you use anything else?' asked Helen.

'Never had to yet.'

They drifted close to shore all afternoon and by teatime had a dozen superb brownies in the boat, averaging around a kilo in weight.

'They're all wild,' Brett told them over a break for a cup of tea. 'We don't stock Arthur's Lake at all, yet we still take 20 000 trout off it each year, and that's completely sustainable. The only limiting factor is the weather; the food just keeps coming and the fish grow like nowhere else I've seen. It's one of the most fantastic stillwater habitats for trout I've come across.'

George drained his cup. 'Another drift?'

They went down to the end of the wind lane, where the trunks of the petrified forest began to poke their heads above the surface, and there they anchored up, about 50 yards from the shore.

'We'll ambush 'em as they come past,' said Brett. 'Every feeding trout in this part of the system will pass us here, so you should be able to fill your boots.'

They caught trout steadily, until Helen had a particularly savage swirl at her Para Dun.

'Jeeees!' shouted Brett. 'Quick, cover him again. That was some fish. There, Helen, he's just to your left.'

Helen cast again just in front of the trout and twitched the Para Dun slightly. Another swirl and this time the fish was firmly hooked, and set off on a powerful run in the opposite direction, away from the boat.

'That's your best today,' cried Brett. 'Don't lose the bugger!'

Helen managed to stop the first run and bring the trout back towards her, but as soon as it came near the boat, it turned back on itself and went away again just as powerfully as before. The difference this time was that it dived deeper and headed more to the left, and she felt that it was on a definite quest of some sort. This was heightened when the fight began to feel peculiar, as though the line was being pulled down to a particular anchor point in the lake rather than the usual random direction of a running fish. Suddenly, everything went solid.

'Has he snagged you?' asked George.

'I think so . . . no, he's moved again . . . now he's stopped. What the hell's going on?'

Brett pointed at the water about 10 yards in front of the boat, where a trout had just swirled and was still plainly visible lying under the surface. It was motionless, apart from the slight tail and fin movements necessary for it to hold station. 'That's your fish I reckon . . . yeah, look at the corner of its mouth, it's your Para Dun.'

Helen's line was still angled deeply into the water and way to the left of the fish. 'He's snagged me round a tree trunk, hasn't he?'

''Fraid so, yeah. Pity, that's a real Arthur's Lake beauty. Look, George, haul in the anchor and let's see if we can't manoeuvre the boat round the trunk and free the bugger.'

George wound in his line and set down his rod, and was giving the fish, now only just under the surface, a final look before reaching for the anchor rope. Then the unbelievable happened. A number of beetles were drifting down the wind lane, past the boat and over the fish. Even though George could see the fly in the trout's jaw, so that it was obviously still tethered to the tree trunk, the fish rose to the surface, slightly to its right so that it gained a little more freedom from the line with the angle change, and sucked in first one and then another beetle before returning to its station just under the surface. Its mouth worked on the insects until they must have been swallowed, because George was watching its every move and nothing was spat out.

'I don't believe that!' cried George, and tapped Brett on the shoulder. 'Did you see. . .?'

'I saw it. I don't believe it either, but I saw it. The bugger's hooked up to Helen's Para Dun but he's still feeding on bloody beetles! Insane!'

George recovered his senses enough to pull in the anchor, and Brett navigated the boat around sunken tree trunks while Helen regained line. After several minutes manoeuvring, the line came free and Helen quickly regained contact with the fish, which, as though rejuvenated by the fresh intake of food, shot off on yet another energetic run and jumped clear of the water.

Helen kept it away from the trunks and finally brought the fish in behind the boat for Brett to net. They measured, photographed and carefully weighed the trout, which pulled the needle round to just less than 4 pounds. Helen then leant over the gunwale and held the fish in the water while it recovered, and let it swim away back into the depths around the watery forest.

That seemed a good enough signal to bring the day's fishing to a close, so they motored back to the lodge and the waiting cold beers.

'Well, that's a first for me,' said Brett. 'I've never even heard of a hooked fish doing that before.'

'So,' said Helen, 'was it feeling pain and just snapping at the beetles out of anger, or was it genuinely feeding?'

George shook his head. 'I was watching it just beforehand. That fish was quietly sitting there, tethered for sure, but it wasn't worried, otherwise it would have been fighting against the tension in the line. I'm *convinced* it came up and took those bugs as food.'

Brett laughed out loud. 'We'll never know for sure, but I'm inclined to agree with you, George. One thing's for certain, though: that's the biggest brown trout you'll see this week, probably the luckiest as well.'

Helen chuckled. 'And definitely the greediest!'

TIGERS, CATS AND ELEPHANTS

Africa offers some of the most atmospheric fishing imaginable. And the proximity of the local wildlife to some of the venues adds a certain spice to the average fishing trip.

I visited Zimbabwe in 1990, mainly to photograph the wildlife, so I only had a telescopic spinning rod with me to cover all fishing eventualities. As to lures, Trevor Housby, the well-known angling writer now sadly no longer with us, had been to Zimbabwe the year before and told me whatever else I did to take loads of mepps spinners, but to replace the treble hooks with singles.

'You'll never hook a tiger on a treble,' he told me. 'Too many teeth! And take more tackle than you'll need. You can't buy anything half decent over there and when you leave, you can give anything left over to the Zimbabweans; you'll be their friend for life.'

I arrived at a camp on the fantastic Zambezi River and, after a dawn game drive, my guide took me out in the smallest boat I've ever fished from. There was just room for the two of us, with him on the outboard and me sitting midships as we trolled a spinner for tigers. There were plenty of islands to weave around, but they couldn't disguise the massive size of the river. They also created a menacing atmosphere, not helped by the guide's running commentary.

'Look, hippos! They're the dangerous ones, you know. They come up underneath and capsize the boat, then when you're struggling in the water, the crocs grab you.' He pointed to the other side of the river, which was Zambia. 'They reckon an average of a person a week gets taken by a croc over there, either fishermen or women coming down to wash their clothes.'

This type of talk is not designed to instil confidence in the visiting angler, especially since the hippos, with their eyes only just visible above the surface, seem to follow your every move, as though waiting for the ideal moment to strike.

'Where are the crocs?' I asked, trying not to sound more than mildly curious.

'Ah, well, you can't see them. They're lying in among the vegetation around the islands and the shoreline. They're there, though; you'd better believe it. Just waiting.'

'Thanks,' I said, then nearly had the rod ripped out of my hands as something akin to an express train hit the mepps and was gone. 'Bloody hell, what was *that*?'

'Tiger. Don't worry, you'll probably only hook into one in ten takes.'

He was right. I wasn't short of obliging tiger fish; I just couldn't get them to stay on the hook. I tried hitting them immediately, giving them time, not striking at all, hard strikes, soft strikes . . . and then one did stick, although I'm not sure I did anything significantly different to make it happen.

The fight was amazing. The tiger, stripes and all, came soaring out of the water, then ran all over the immediate Zambezi, leaping plenty and trying to dive under the boat when it came close enough. Just as quickly as the acrobatics had started, the fish gave up and was easy enough to draw to the net. As soon as it hit the bottom of the boat, the mepps fell out of its mouth.

'That's 3 kilos, about $6^{1}/_{2}$ pounds,' said my guide, shaking my hand. 'Nice fish. Good size for eating.'

We fished on until mid-afternoon and I had a couple more, smaller tigers, but I must have missed another dozen. Either there was one Houdini fish continually hitting the spinner or the Zambezi is full of tiger fish. At least, it was then. It would be interesting to know whether the tiger population survived the locals' need for protein during Zimbabwe's 'difficult' years.

We went back to the camp and transferred to a big catamaran, where more guests boarded and we motored slowly upstream to wait for the evening arrival of the elephants to drink from the river. While we waited, we fished on the bottom with bait and caught a few bream. Then I had a slow draw of a take that was different from anything else I had felt thus far in Africa. I struck and everything went solid, then the fish moved away from the boat ever so sedately, as though all the pressure I was putting on it was of no consequence at all.

'Catfish!' the guide called out. 'You've hooked a bloody great catfish, you lucky so and so.'

I didn't feel all that lucky, as my rod was totally inadequate for the fight. The fish just kept swimming towards Zambia and nothing I did made the slightest difference to it; it didn't deviate once from its course.

'Try stopping it before it gets to the middle,' said the guide optimistically. 'The current's too strong out there and you'll never hold it.'

'Er ... slight problem on that front,' I suggested. 'I can't stop it in here, let alone out there.'

The fish did turn, miraculously, and come back to the boat, but I rather fancy it did so just to give me hope. Either that or it had no idea it was actually hooked, or perhaps it wanted to watch the elephants as well.

'How big do the catfish go in here?' I asked, looking warily at the crazy bend in the telescopic rod.

'Huge. I reckon that one might be 50, maybe 100,' said the guide.

'If it's only 50 pounds, I might have a chance if we stay out all night.'

'I meant *kilos*.'

I was trying to think of a suitable riposte to that when the fish turned and powered away from us again. I wound down the drag on the fixed-spool reel, for all the good that would do, and just hung on. The catfish went further this time and with more purpose, reaching the faster current near the middle of the channel before turning right and heading for Victoria Falls.

'Point your rod straight at it,' said one of the others on the boat. 'It's either shit or bust with that thing now.'

He was right, and I did. It kept pulling line off the reel even then, until the pressure became too much and everything went slack. I reeled in and was surprised that I still had my tackle intact; except that the hook had pulled out straight. I hadn't even seen the fish, but I was pretty certain it had been the biggest thing I had ever hooked, either at sea or in fresh water. Even though I hadn't expected to land it, losing it was gut wrenching.

'Bad luck,' said the guide.

I shrugged and forced out a laugh. 'No problem, I'll bring the big-game gear next time.'

As evening draws on, the Zambezi takes on an almost primaeval atmosphere, and I had a rather depressing feeling in my stomach that the river wasn't prepared to give up any more of its inhabitants to a visiting Englishman; certainly not its monsters. It actually felt quite frightening at that point: the size of the river, together with the knowledge of what lay concealed beneath the blackened water, whether mammal, reptile or fish. There was a brooding grandeur to the place that made me feel very insignificant.

Thank goodness for elephants! There was a shout from someone at the other end of the boat and I turned to see a big herd emerge from the trees. The young ones led the charge, running as fast as their tired legs would carry them and practically diving into the river in their frenzy to drink. The older animals seemed more cautious, especially with us humans watching them from the cat, which the guide had gently driven into the beach so that we were stationary. But then the whole herd reached the river. We were literally surrounded by drinking elephants and it was one of the most amazing wildlife spectacles I have ever seen. The cold box was opened and I was handed a freezing bottle of beer, at which point I forgot about tiger fish escape artists and mammoth catfish and enjoyed the treat of being around those wonderful creatures. Not for the first time, I wondered at the privilege offered to us fishermen by nature, just by being on the riverbank at times like that. I doubt if my lost catfish will fade from the memory, but I'm certain the elephants never will.

Back at the camp, showered and cleanly clothed, we assembled at the bar for pre-dinner drinks and there was the tiger fish, baked and the skin taken off. Instead of eating nuts or olives, we used our fingers, African style, to pick up chunks of tiger fish from between the bones. It tasted so good in that atmosphere, with the barbeque and wood-smoke smells on the air.

They say that Africa gets into your blood and that you feel compelled to return. I will do one day, and I'll take a modern travel rod with some more backbone, because I want a chance again at a truly wild freshwater fish of the size my imagination tells me that catfish was.

And while I'm about it, I'll get some advice on how to improve the hook-up rate on those ruddy tiger fish as well.

CASCADES AND THE FRENCH LINE FISHERMAN

Does this extraordinary event support the premise that fish fight against pressure on the line rather than any pain they might feel on the hook?

I've been told by various people that if when playing a salmon you take pressure off the fish and give it slack line, it will return to its lie and remain quiet, seemingly unaware that it is still hooked. I've never had the confidence to try this experiment myself, being too scared of losing the few salmon I actually manage to hook. However, at the end of one extraordinary day on a Scottish river, I had an insight into what they were talking about.

I was fishing on the Spey, upstream from Aberlour, and had spent most of the morning hearing news via Sam, the ghillie, that everyone else bar me seemed to have caught fish. While not an unusual occurrence, it is always slightly worrying that other people are doing something I must be missing. I had just started fishing the head of what I'd been told was the least promising pool on the upper beat, with lunchtime beckoning, and was wondering what I was doing wrong. Sam had told me in the morning not to bother with Cascade flies; he hated them and was convinced a Willie Gunn was better on the Spey. Having tried most other flies during the morning, I now had on a Cascade as a last resort.

I remember thinking vaguely that it was a pity this pool wasn't producing fish, because the line was coming round beautifully, at just the right pace, and I reckoned every cast was worthy of a thunderous take. I had just cast again and the fly was mid-channel, when I had a lovely solid draw on the line and was into a fresh springer that turned out to be about 8 pounds. No one was around, so I kept the fish in the water, gently holding its tail wrist with one hand while photographing it with my waterproof camera in the other. I supported it just off the current while it revived and watched it swim back into the pool.

I arrived at the lodge for lunch with a bit more confidence that I was doing something right for a change, and had a laugh with Sam about the Cascade.

'Fluke!' he said. 'It would have taken a Willie Gunn just as well.'

We were having lunch when someone remarked that a squirrel was pinching nuts from the bird table. This is a fairly regular occurrence at home, so I didn't get too excited, until I realised that it was a red squirrel. I then became the butt of people's jokes as I went outside and assumed a secret commando-type approach to the bird table, using trees as cover and taking photographs every few yards so that I captured increasingly larger images of the squirrel. I managed to get quite close before it decided I was a threat to its existence and scampered off into the upper branches of a Scots Pine.

Despite the humorous backchat from the rest of the party, all of whom were used to seeing red squirrels because they lived in Scotland or northern England, watching one that day was an event for me. I grew up with red squirrels as a boy, taking them totally for granted and laughing at my father forever chasing them out of the fruit trees in our garden. Before my Spey sighting, however, I hadn't seen one in the flesh for 30 years, which just goes to prove how a species can move from abundance to rarity in the blink of an evolutionary eye, especially if helped on its way by an alien invader such as the grey squirrel. I proceeded to bore the rest of the party over the lunch table about this red versus grey battle, and how similar it was to what was happening with alien aquatic species up and down our river systems.

After lunch, my host James showed me the lower beat. There were two main pools and two smaller pots, one of which, he said, hardly ever produced a fish, but it was worth half a dozen casts on the way through. So I went into the pot and second cast, another deep, solid draw and I landed a 10-pounder. I photographed that one too, including a close-up of its mouth with the Cascade beside it, just to rub it into Sam when I saw him again. I returned the fish and went on to the boat pool, feeling quietly smug about life.

'Fish the pool down hard for about 50 yards,' my host had told me. 'There's a bit right at the bottom that sometimes holds a fish, but it's only worth a couple of casts.'

I fished the main pool and didn't get a sniff. Again I went into the unproductive water, and immediately had a savage take on the Cascade, the fish racing off towards the foot bridge at Aberlour. Unfortunately, that was the last I saw of it, because we parted company just after the backing appeared through the top ring, so my hopes of a hat-trick in the day from unpromising lies were dashed.

I returned to the top of the lower beat, to a superb pool that was fishing the best of the whole fishery. A party of Frenchmen were on the other bank and they had been catching salmon hand over fist for the past couple of days. The main taking zone was at the bottom of the pool, and I was slowly making my way down, observing my etiquette and not impeding my opposite number on the other bank, who was some little way ahead of me. Part of the agreement between the two fisheries was that neither side would wade too far into the river, so protecting the fish from unnecessary disturbance and giving everyone the best chance of catching something. I was rather miffed, therefore, to see a Frenchman further over than normal, poking even deeper into the channel with his 15-foot rod, as though trying to reach something with it. I couldn't understand what he was doing, especially as his ghillie was standing on the bank watching and doing nothing to stop him. This wasn't playing the game, I decided.

Then the Frenchman picked the tip of his rod out of the water, and it looked as though he was trying to lift a cream-coloured cord that must have been lying under the surface. I immediately thought back to the film *Bridge over the River Kwai*, when the commandos wake up in the morning and find that the river has dropped in the night, exposing the cable they laid along the river-bed to the explosive charges under the bridge. It looked just like that: cord hitched over the rod tip and disappearing back below the surface in both up and down-stream directions. There was obviously a significant length of whatever it was.

The Frenchman used the tip of his rod with great dexterity, nearly falling in a couple of times but finally managing to grab the cord in his hand. He gingerly made his way to the shore and passed it to the ghillie, who proceeded to pull in the upstream end while the Frenchman climbed out of the river and frantically stripped all the fly line off his reel onto the grass.

I waded a little quicker now, fascinated by what was happening. I saw the Frenchman hand his rod to the ghillie, who attached the cord to the reel. It was then I realised that it was obviously a fly line that had been discarded in the river. The rod was given back to the Frenchman, who returned to the water and reeled in the slack line before beginning to pump at a weight on the end.

I was quite close by this time and it soon became obvious that he was playing a fish. It was a spirited fight from the salmon, charging off on a couple of decent runs and taking some time to subdue before he managed to bring it to the net. I'm delighted to say that, even though we knew his party had killed several salmon up to that point, this one was released back to the river. If ever a fish deserved it, that one did. Apparently it had been hooked the previous evening, and had run down the pool with such power that the whole fly line had been ripped off the reel and then the backing braid had snapped; or, more likely, the knot had come undone. The fish had gone back to its lie and, presumably, stayed there with the hook still in its mouth for nearly 24 hours before being reattached to the Frenchman and continuing the battle.

The final twist to this story is that I shouted my congratulations across to the Frenchman and the ghillie, and said that nobody would believe them when they tried to tell their story. Little did I know I would soon get this opportunity to publish it myself.

PART FIVE

Extraordinary Tales

THE OBNOXIOUS MAJOR

Ghillies have been used to dealing with difficult clients ever since their profession was invented. Each has their own way of handling arrogant anglers while staying within the rules of bank-side etiquette, but they can only be pushed so far.

G hillies can be wonderful characters, and they can also be as dour as a dreek Scottish weather event. Get them onside and they can help you catch fish where you would otherwise struggle, but the flipside is that you upset them at your peril. One such incident from the River Lochy, on Scotland's west coast, started with an arrogant fishing guest making dictatorial demands and culminated in obedience to the letter, and just about as ignominious an end as it was possible to conjure up.

Back in the 1950s, when salmon were plentiful in Scottish rivers, it was common practice for anglers to catch so many fish that they had contracts with Billingsgate dealers. They would send wooden boxes full of salmon down on the train to London at the end of each day. In retrospect this did little for conservation, but in many cases it paid for entire fishing trips.

Back to the Lochy, sometime in the mid-1950s. The fishing guest was a Major Jackson, at least for the purposes of this tale, and the ghillie answered to Murdo. So it was that Murdo met Jackson on the banks of the Lochy at 9 o'clock on a Monday morning. The weather was perfect, with good cloud cover, excellent visibility and a fresh atmosphere. It was perfect for salmon fishing and it was quite obvious that there were salmon in the river: they were showing all over the pool and Jackson was impatient to get started.

'Now, Murdo, whatever else you do for me this week, make sure that you put my fish on the 5 o'clock train each evening. D'you understand?'

'Whatever you say, Major Jackson.'

'Your job is to box them up, ice them down for the journey and then get them on that ruddy train. Clear?'

'Clear as day, Major Jackson. Can I suggest the Munro killer this morning?'

'I always fish a blue charm! There's my box; I've every size we'll need, on singles and trebles, so make sure you look after them. Now, where do I start on this pool?'

'Just follow me, Major Jackson.'

Jackson followed Murdo up the bank. 'And one more thing. I don't want any fish with holes in their bodies; it affects the price terribly. So no gaffs: all fish must be carefully netted, do you understand?'

'Quite understood, Major Jackson,' said Murdo patiently. He met all kinds on the riverbank, but this one was beginning to take the biscuit. He could quite cheerfully lure him into a deep hole and let him drown; he had a fleeting image of the major's head sinking into the peaty water, that pompous little moustache twitching wildly in panic as he disappeared. He grinned to himself at that, but then they were at the head of the pool and he was preparing the major's rod for the first cast.

'The best lie is just over. . .'

'I know how to fish, Murdo. No need to fuss, man.'

Infuriatingly, the major was as good as his word. Murdo hated to admit it, but the bloody man could fish. He cast lightly and waded sensitively, so that he didn't disturb the fish he covered. Murdo wished every guest he looked after was as knowledgeable about the ways of salmon as this man, even though he had a polluted character to go with it. And it paid off, too. On only his fourth cast, before he had hardly had time to settle into a rhythm, the rod tip dipped and he was into a beautiful silver 6-pound grilse.

Murdo couldn't believe how the major played his salmon. Most fishermen were so desperate to make sure they landed their fish that they tended to be over-cautious, especially with the first one of the week. Not so Major Jackson. He hardly allowed the fish to run, but rather took all the energy out of it by holding it close on a short line and an unusually thick leader. It seemed to work, though, because the fish was in Murdo's net within two minutes and swiftly despatched with a heavy wooden priest.

For the first time this morning, Jackson actually smiled, tweaking his moustache as he did. 'That's one for the 5 o'clock, Murdo, eh?'

'Certainly is, sir.'

Jackson continued to catch fish all morning. He seemed instinctively to know where the best lies were, and as often as not a fish would be hooked. The other remarkable thing was how few fish he lost. As unlikely as it seemed, the short-line policy seemed to work. They were hooked, played, netted and killed in as quick a time as Murdo had ever witnessed. Major Jackson was more like a fish merchant than an angler; he seemed interested only in the money he would make down in London, rather than any pleasure he was gaining from his sport.

Then something happened for which Murdo had been waiting the full seven years he had been working on the river. The major's fly came round on a freshly oiled line that was floating high on the surface and the most enormous salmon head and tailed right behind it. The line straightened, the major lifted his rod and the fish was on.

'For God's sake, sir, let this one run, it's bloody...'

'Yes, I can see what size it is for myself, thank you, Murdo.'

Murdo shut up and watched in awe as the fish bored deep, ran first upstream, then down towards the tail of the pool, and then leapt, not completely clear of the water, but far enough to get a good idea of the size.

'Jeeesuuus!' muttered Murdo under his breath. 'That's 40 pounds of salmon if ever I saw it.'

'A bit coloured, isn't it?'

'Perhaps not as fresh as some, but it's not too bad, sir.'

The major played it well and patiently, which was surprising after this morning's performance. This would be the fish of Murdo's career, he knew that for certain, the one he would remember into his old age and tell his grandchildren about. And if he had to choose an angler to be on the other end right now, he would look no further than Major Jackson. He was, without question, the very best man for the job.

'How long's it been, Murdo?'

'About 20 minutes, Major. He must be getting tired now.'

'It doesn't feel like it, and I keep seeing these fresh fish moving through.'

Murdo wasn't quite sure what he meant by that. What the hell had grilse to do with it when he was playing such a great fish? Then, quite suddenly, the major took hold of the line with his left hand and gave it a vicious jerk.

Murdo stared at him and for a moment forgot his position. 'What the hell are you doing, Major?'

'I'm bored with this and I'm missing the chance of catching saleable fish. No one wants to buy a coloured lump like this; I need more grilse.'

'But... Major Jackson!'

He was too late. The major had given the line an even stronger yank this time and the leader had broken just above the fly. The salmon came to the surface, rolled over once to show the depth on its magnificent, autumnal-coloured flank, and then it was gone.

Murdo could only stand in complete bewilderment and stare at Jackson. In that moment, he felt as though he had never hated anyone quite as much. Surely no genuine fisherman could ever have done what this man just had? If he hadn't seen it with his own eyes, Murdo would have said it was inconceivable.

'Come on, man, *wake up*! Tie me on another size 10 treble and let's get some more grilse on the bank. And don't leave it too late to catch that train.'

Murdo found an excuse in the afternoon to go and make sure the other guests and their ghillies were happy. Really, he just wanted to be out of the major's sight. He still felt numb.

Half an hour later, he returned to where the major should have been, but he wasn't. Perhaps he had hooked that mighty fish again, which had made him late coming down to the lower pool. Murdo walked up the bank, past the shallow riffle and up to the pool where he had left Jackson. And there he still was, except that he was now lying face down in the water, absolutely still.

Murdo ran up to help the major, but one look at his staring eyes confirmed that he was stone dead. He was still holding the rod and the line was moving about, heading down into the middle of the pool. Murdo prised the rod from Jackson's hands and quickly landed an exhausted grilse; it had obviously been fighting the dead man for some time.

Murdo looked at his watch. If he was going to obey orders and get to that train on time, he had to leave with the fish so that he could box and ice them and drive over to the station. No time to deal with the major; it looked like a massive heart attack had done that already.

Murdo would have to come back later and see to him, but at least the Billingsgate contract would have been honoured, and that was all that seemed to have mattered around there today.

DON'T FOOL WITH
THE JOKER!

It can be dangerous to try to upstage a professional jester. The law of unintended consequences can sometimes bite you back with a vengeance.

Ron Simmons was one of angling's great practical jokers. Sadly no longer around to tell the host of outrageous stories for which he was legendary, some of which were even vaguely true, he could, with the best of intentions, be mercilessly cruel to the unwary. Examples of his exploits included putting lugworms in someone's sandwiches when they weren't looking and exploding into fits of laughter as the first bite sank into the offending snack. Then there was the old schoolboy trick of putting salt in tea rather than sugar and, conversely, shaking sugar over a friend's fish and chips in the pub on the way home. And having breakfast at his house before a trip was always a lottery, especially if boiled eggs were on the menu: they could be anything from rock solid to raw, depending on his mood that morning.

The one saving grace was that Ron was extremely amiable and it was difficult to be mad at him for long. He never let anyone suffer from his joking and would always make sure that sandwiches, tea, fish and chips and whatever else were swiftly replaced from his own wallet. Even when he slipped a bag of frozen squid into Terry's bag at the end of a day's fishing on the pier, knowing that Terry wouldn't be out again for a few weeks and the squid would defrost and slowly putrefy, he made sure he had a new bag ready to hand over when the inevitable accusation flew his way.

Then there was the time he was out on a boat trip and Frank caught a magnificent 10-pound turbot, the first of its species any of the party had ever landed. On the spur of the moment, Ron invited Terry and Frank and their wives for supper the next evening, an invitation they immediately accepted. When no one was looking, Ron quietly whipped the turbot out of Frank's polystyrene box, replaced it with half a dozen dogfish to make up the weight, covered them with crushed ice and put the lid back on. Frank left the boat proudly clutching his boxed catch, and was only placated the following evening when Ron's wife produced the most superb turbot dish; she, of course, having been fooled into believing that this was the first turbot her husband had ever caught.

A few weeks later, Frank and Terry decided it was high time they repaid Ron in kind. They were fishing from Chesil Beach, a long, thin strand of shingle along Dorset's Jurassic coast in southern England. They each had two rods, one to throw out as far as they could with ragworm baits in the hope of a decent plaice or black bream, the other for fishing closer in with squid, trying to intercept any bass that might be feeding in the breakers. They didn't often hook bass there, but when they did, it was usually a decent one, Frank having caught the record for the trio a couple of years earlier with a fish of just under 6 pounds.

They were quite optimistic that morning, as the weather had been rough up until a couple of days before but now the water was clearing, with enough of a swell to create some decent surf in the breakers. The bream and flatties should be feeding out in the deeper water, and it was an ideal sea state for a marauding bass to pick up one of the whole calamari squid rolling around in their path, about 30 yards off the beach.

Frank and Terry hadn't hatched any special plan to pay Ron back; it was just that, as he had walked some distance away to answer a call of nature at that particular moment, they were presented with an unusual opportunity to do something. Booby trapping his fishing box or sabotaging his sandwiches were possibilities, but they weren't particularly original and Ron definitely deserved more than that.

'Quick, think of something,' said Frank. 'He'll be back in a minute.'

'I can't. You think of something.'

'I'm no good at practical jokes. I don't have Ron's warped sense of humour.'

'What about reeling in his line and tying a bloody great rock to it?'

'Then what? You can't cast a rock back out to sea, can you?'

'True. Hey, I know.' Terry started rummaging around in his tackle box. 'I've got a perk in here somewhere. I bought it for that boat trip last month and never used it. There you go.' He pulled out a long, silver-coloured and vaguely fish-shaped metal tube, with a swivel at one end and a large treble hook at the other.

'How heavy is it?' asked Frank.

'About a pound, I should think.'

'Will his rod be able to cast it?'

'Yeah, if we're careful. And with that shape on the perk, it'll feel like it's wriggling when he winds it in. He's sure to think he's caught something.'

'Right, hurry up, then, he won't be long.'

Terry quickly wound in Ron's flattie rod, cut off the end tackle at the swivel and tied on the perk. After a swift look up the beach to make sure Ron wasn't watching, he walked to the edge of the surf, worked up a gentle pendulum and then smoothly cast the perk straight out in front of him. It landed with a splash about 80 yards away.

Ron was soon sauntering back up the beach, hands in pockets and whistling softly. 'Anything doing?' he asked when he reached them.

'Yeah, you had one good knock just now,' Frank said.

'Really? Which rod?'

'That one. Don't think it was a bream, looked more like a plaice having a nibble.'

'There, it went again,' said Terry.

'I didn't see anything,' said Ron.

'Definitely!' said Frank. 'Just a tap, tap on the tip.'

'I'd better take a look then.'

Ron picked up the beachcaster, struck solidly at whatever was out there and began to reel in. 'Yeah, you're right!'

'Any size?' asked Terry, trying not to laugh.

'Dunno yet. Reasonable flattie, I'd say.'

'Bet it's not as big as my turbot,' muttered Frank.

'Maybe not, but I haven't caught a decent plaice yet this year,' stated Ron, getting visibly excited as the 'fish' came closer. 'Hey, it really kicked, then. Maybe it's bigger than I thought.'

'You're in the surf now,' Terry reminded him, forcing himself to keep a straight face. 'It's bound to feel heavier in the turbulence.'

Ron nodded. 'Yeah, I suppose so. Hey, what's so funny, Frank?'

'No. . . nothing!' stammered Frank. 'Just pleased you've caught something, that's all.'

'What's going on here?' demanded Ron. 'I know you two, and something's. . . frigging hell!'

The perk had been no more than 10 yards out when the rod tip was pulled down violently and line ripped off the spool against the drag and scythed away through the surf. Whatever was on the other end was heading resolutely towards Portland Bill.

Terry stared open mouthed. 'What the hell. . .?'

'Damn bass must have taken the fish!' Ron shouted. 'I can't hardly hold the thing, it's enormous!'

The fish kept close in, as though it was happier in the surf than out deeper, but the extra pressure on the line from the pounding swell made the fight much more dramatic. Terry had never seen a beachcaster bounce around as much as Ron's was doing right then, and he was certain the line would give at any moment, or the hook would be torn out of the fish. He couldn't believe the drama that was unfurling in front of him. What size of fish had hit a perk designed to catch ruddy great cod and ling over a wreck, for goodness' sake?

The fish changed its mind and headed for deeper water.

'Let it stay out there for a bit,' Terry advised, completely taken over by the fight, even though he was dreading the ribbing that would come his way when Ron discovered the reality of the situation. 'Less chance of losing him out there.'

Ron nodded. 'I wonder what the fish was that he took. It's not like a bass to hit a flatfish, is it? Perhaps it was a bream after all.'

'Just concentrate on landing the bloody thing,' Terry interrupted. 'It's probably the biggest bass you'll ever hook, you jammy sod!'

It was about 15 minutes later that Ron finally had the fish under some sort of control, at the furthest edge of the surf. He waited for a swell to come in, then walked quickly backwards up the beach, reeling in as he went. As the surf receded, a massive bass was left stranded on dry land, the treble hook lodged firmly in its jaws and the unmistakable shape of the perk lying alongside.

Terry ran down, grabbed hold of the bass through the gills and, ignoring the stabs of pain from the spines, dragged the fish clear of the water and up onto a higher level of beach.

'Frigging. . .' Ron's voice tailed off.

'Big, isn't it?' was all Frank could say.

'Er, lads, what's that bloody great thing sticking out of its mouth?'

'It's a long story. . .'

Terry's worst fears were realised. He and Frank were ribbed mercilessly for the rest of Ron's all too brief life after that. For the record, the fish went 12¾ pounds, by far the biggest bass any of them had ever caught, or had ever seen, come to that.

As for Terry and Frank, they were still planning that one infallible plan to get their own back, right until the end. Sadly, they ran out of time.

CBA POT

You can't catch fish unless your line is in the water. However uninspiring the conditions may be, it's always worth having a go. You never know, you might even become responsible for naming a new pool.

Some salmon pools bear the surnames of personalities who fished them in the past, while others relate to terrestrial features: Black Rock, Bridge, Farm and the like. The discovery of a new pool is very rare, even after major flood events. The topography of existing pools may change dramatically when the river is in particularly heavy spate, but seldom does such a torrent create completely new holding places for fish. So the naming of a new pool is exceptional these days, but not unheard of.

A few years ago, something amazing happened in the north east of England that spawned just such a naming ceremony. A small group of fishers made their annual pilgrimage to the Coquet, a small but beautiful river in Northumberland that, on its day, can provide tremendous sport for salmon and trout anglers. Actually, not all the party arrived at the same time: John and Mike started fishing on the Monday, but Robin was unable to arrive until the Tuesday, being tied up with last-minute meetings that he couldn't afford to miss.

Monday was hot and sultry and, with a lack of rainfall for weeks before, the river was desperately low and beginning to show its bones. There were now rocks that John and Mike hadn't seen before and the riffles between pools were beginning to look rather feeble. Sea trout might run them and the smaller grilse perhaps, but that was always assuming there was enough fresh water to entice them off the tide and away from the feeding seals.

Monday was spent more in hope than expectation. They covered all the pools meticulously, but the breaks between fishing for a beer and a chat became longer and longer as the day wore on. Just sitting around was enough to produce a sweat, and it was obvious that the only event likely to liven up both the weather conditions and the fishing was a decent thunderstorm. Even the resident brown trout were reluctant to rise to the sporadic hatches of fly, and it seemed as though all things environmental were in abeyance. Dinner was taken early and the malt whisky in the bar became a more attractive proposition than flogging the pools after dark in the vain hope of enticing a sea trout to take.

John and Mike made a tardy appearance at the breakfast table.

'Did you hear the thunder in the night?' asked their landlady.

'Er. . . no,' replied John, conscious of the fact that only a minor earthquake would have roused him from his slumbers once he had actually made it to bed. 'Any rain to go with it?'

'Yes, it was violent for a while. It's beaten up my roses outside, but it probably wasn't enough for you fishermen. You're never satisfied, are you? You're worse than farmers, you lot, with your weather requirements. It's never quite what you want.'

John nodded. 'True.' His heart was beating slightly faster, though, and he exchanged glances with Mike. Any rain was better than nothing.

The air was slightly fresher as they tackled up beside the cars, but they still weren't ideal conditions for fishing. The hotel barometer had remained at low pressure and experience had shown them that salmon rarely took until the dial began to rise. Still, they started at the top of the beat and worked their way down, taking it in turns to use the fly rod and then the spinner. The river was definitely fuller than it had been the previous day, but it still wasn't anywhere near ideal height and the rain had coloured the water.

They spent the rest of the morning covering every metre of every pool, but nothing took either lure and only the very occasional fish splashed on the surface to show that anything was living in the river at all. If they hadn't had days like this hundreds of times over the past 20 years, it might have been soul destroying. As it was, they were experienced salmon fishers and had seen it all before. It came with the package if you hunted migratory fish.

At about 1 o'clock they stopped to eat their packed lunches, perched high above the river on a rocky outcrop from where, had there been a reasonable number of fish, they could have seen them running through the broken water below them. They had sat there many times before and watched pods of grilse splash through on their way upstream, but today it was dead. An elongated lunchtime session progressed into mid-afternoon, with plenty of chat about how much better the fishing had been there in years past.

The pair of them were still on their rock, drinking the last of their coffee, when Robin arrived, frustrated that he had missed so much fishing time and eager to get started, especially with the thought that the rain from last night must have freshened up the river.

'How are you doing?' he asked brightly.

'Rubbish!' replied Mike. 'Not even a touch.'

'Well, you won't catch anything sulking up here,' retorted Robin. 'A salmon won't take if you haven't got a line in the water.'

'We've covered the whole ruddy fishery, every inch of it. We need fresher air.'

'You two are too bloody scientific! What you don't realise is that the salmon haven't read the same books as you. Come on, let's get fishing.'

'You go on, we'll watch you.'

Robin sighed. 'All right, I'll go and start up at the top. Why don't you two have another go here? Look, down there for instance, there's a likely-looking pot between those two rocks.'

'What? No one fishes down there. It isn't even a pool. Anything running the river goes straight through this water and doesn't stop until it gets to the beat above us.'

'Right, so you haven't fished down there today?'

'We haven't fished there ever,' said John patiently.

'Okay, but just have one go. You won't know if you don't try.'

'Look, you do it,' said Mike. 'We can't be arsed.'

'All right, you stay here and be moribund. I'll climb down and do it. Someone's got to show willing.'

Robin made his way gingerly down the cliff path and arrived just above the big rock at the top of the run. There was another, smaller boulder about 20 yards below and he was quite right: at this height of water, you could see there was a small pot that might conceivably hold a fish, if there were any fish to hold.

Robin threw a couple of speculative short casts, presumably in case anything was holding just in front of him. From their vantage point, Mike and John could have told him there was nothing there. They could see every pebble on the bottom, and fish there weren't.

Robin extended the casts, covering the more broken water just above the pot. It wasn't possible to see whether there were fish there, but it was highly unlikely. Next time the fly went right into the pot, landing equidistant between the two stones. Robin put an immediate upstream mend in the line and the silver ally's shrimp came across at a perfect speed and angle; they could watch every inch of its progress from up on the cliff.

They also saw the salmon appear out of the pot, almost in slow motion as it followed the fly, seemingly transfixed by this alien being in its solitary lair. Just as the fly slowed out of the current, the fish took it and, with a flick of its head, rolled away to return to its lie.

Robin tightened into the salmon, and then let out the most unholy yell of delight. 'Told you!'

'I do not flaming *believe* it!' roared John. 'Tell me this isn't happening, for God's sake!'

'I'm afraid it is. Come on, let's go and help the jammy sod!'

'We'll never hear the end of this, you know? He'll be insufferable for the rest of the week.'

The fish was quite coloured, having been in the river for perhaps three or four weeks. Robin played it expertly, landed it, had his photograph taken and then returned it unharmed to the river, whereupon it swam serenely back into the pot. Now came the time John and Mike had been dreading.

'Just shows, you doesn't it?' crowed Robin. 'A bit of effort, and a willingness to experiment, and then...'

'Yes, alright, don't rub it in,' said Mike in a resigned tone. 'You realise we've a job to do now, don't you?'

Robin frowned. 'What?'

'This isn't a recognised pool. We need to name it.'

'How about *Robin's Pot*?' Robin suggested modestly.

'I've got a better idea,' said John.

'What?'

John took out his hip flask and poured a few drops of whisky into the water. 'I name this place the CBA Pot.'

Robin's frown deepened. 'CBA?'

'Can't Be Arsed,' said John.

The name has stuck. And when the water is low on the Coquet, the threesome wouldn't dream of fishing without a few casts in the CBA Pot; even though, to their knowledge, it hasn't produced another fish from that day to this!

ANCHORS AND LEMONADE

Preparation is all well and good until something happens for which you could not possibly have prepared. And when the person in charge starts to panic, it is time to think on your feet – fast!

Fly fishing for bonefish, tarpon and the many other exotic species found in the beautiful clear waters of the Caribbean and Indian Ocean exploded in popularity during the last couple of decades of the twentieth century. Great fun though saltwater fly-fishing is, exponents still occasionally like to take time out and revert to the old methods of bait or surface lure fishing with poppers for bigger specimens, such as barracuda, billfish or one of the all-time favourite quarries, giant trevally. Trevally, pound for pound, have a reputation for being one of the hardest fighting fish in the sea.

Steve was on Alphonse in the Indian Ocean. He decided to ask his boatman whether they could venture out beyond the reef into slightly deeper water. He had been down to the fish market early the previous morning and seen some of the boxes being landed. There were species there that never came onto the flats where he had been stalking bone fish, and he felt an urge to try to catch some of them. In particular, the giant trevally looked a perfect target. He had heard people talk about how hard they fought and he fancied having a crack at them. He might not get another chance for years and it would be criminal to pass up this opportunity while he had it.

His guide wasn't exactly enthusiastic. Actually, Steve suspected that this was more to do with taking the boat beyond the reef, and out of the boatman's comfort zone, than with what species they were hunting. But a couple of crumpled banknotes in his shirt top pocket sealed the deal and they duly motored out beyond the reef and began fishing around the rocks outside the bay.

Steve's first trevally was an amazing experience. The popper lure streaked across the surface and, all of a sudden, a massive head and shoulders appeared from beneath the waves, shadowed the popper for a few seconds and then engulfed it. Whereas the bonefish only had one way to fight in the shallow flats, by running straight out towards the edge of the reef at rapid speed, the trevally had the third dimension of deep water in which to charge around. The power was incredible, stripping line off the multiplier spool and boring away with incredible stamina. It took upwards of 20 minutes to bring it close enough to the boat to tail.

'Great fish,' cried the boatman. 'It's 20 kilos or 44 pounds, easy.' At least he looked happier now as he lifted the fish into the boat and extracted the popper from its mouth. Steve picked up the giant trevally, photographs were taken and then he carefully returned it to the water to swim sedately away towards the rocks.

Steve took another couple of smaller giant trevallies and was playing a fourth fish. He hadn't seen it yet and wasn't convinced it was a trevally. It was definitely the smallest fish he had hooked so far and wasn't fighting with the same gusto as the others. He began to bully it towards the surface, then everything went solid on him, as though the fish had snagged him on an obstruction of some kind.

'I think he's taken me into the rocks.'

'No rocks here; not that shallow, anyway. Hey, what's happening?'

The solid 'rock' had now woken up and Steve's rod had bounced over into a solid arc pointing straight down into the water. Line came off the multiplier at ever increasing speed, and soon the fish was into a full run, a bit like a giant trevally but much heavier.

'It's a fish!' cried Steve, 'and not the one I hooked first time round. Would a big trevally take a smaller fish?'

The boatman looked doubtful and apprehensive at the same time. 'Not unless it's the biggest one I've ever seen. That's some fish you're playing there.'

Steve let it run for a while, occasionally winning line back and losing it again just as quickly. The tackle wasn't really up to the job, but he was patient, and slowly he began to gain control. Even so, it was probably an hour or more before they saw the first glimpse of the fish appearing below them in the turquoise water.

'What is it?' Steve asked, peering through his fishing glasses.

There was silence for a few moment, and then the boatman sucked in his breath. 'Shark – it's a bloody shark!'

From his tone of voice, Steve quickly deduced that his right-hand man was not a great fan of sharks. In fact, he sounded downright scared, which did not bode well for handling a large shark from a small boat. This was confirmed when the fish surfaced, whereupon Steve had the distinct impression that, had there been more room in the boat, the boatman would almost certainly have been trying to hide behind him. He pulled the fish alongside.

'Lemon shark,' stated the boatman.

'They're not particularly dangerous, are they?'

'All sharks dangerous!'

There was no equipment in the boat for handling large fish. Steve wouldn't allow a gaff anyway, because all his fish went back alive, unless they specifically wanted one to eat, a category the lemon shark did not fit into. The only aid they had was the boatman's gloves.

'Can you grab its tail?' Steve asked, deciding that was the best place for the boatman, it being furthest away from the teeth end.

'No way I'm touching any part of that fish!'

'You've *got* to help somehow. I can't handle a 6-foot shark on my own!'

The boatman merely shook his head and tried to move even further away.

Steve's brain went into overdrive. 'Okay. Look, you take the rod and leave the rest to me.'

The boatman didn't look too happy about this plan either, but it must have seemed the least dangerous option for him, so he gingerly took the rod, although he handled it as though it was a live bomb. Steve grabbed the anchor from the bows and dragged it back amidships. He took hold of the rope, lunged at the rear end of the shark and managed to wrap the rope around its tail wrist before it had a chance to react.

All hell let lose, with Steve clinging onto the rope, leaning back with all his might and his feet braced against the gunwale, as the shark went into a tail-beating frenzy that threatened to smash the little boat to pieces. The boatman cried out in alarm but, mercifully, kept his cool enough to hold onto the rod and control the shark's writhing head. They were both soaked to the skin in seconds.

Steve soon realised that they were going nowhere with this strategy. While the shark was well and truly tailed, the lure was still embedded in its jaw and the chances of the boatman offering to free it were non-existent. Steve waited until the fish had quietened down a bit.

'Can you hand me the rod and take over on the rope?' he enquired cautiously.

The boatman eyed the shark suspiciously, thought about this for a few moments but then slowly handed the rod to Steve, who for a second or two was left holding the rope in one hand and the rod in the other. Fortunately, the shark didn't realise that its chance for freedom had momentarily arrived, and it kept reasonably quiet while the boatman moved behind Steve and gingerly took the rope off him.

Steve moved up to the head of the fish and wondered how he was ever going to remove the treble hook. It was a minor miracle that it had stayed put anyway, but the size of the lure and the fact that it was only hooked in the outside jaw gristle meant that the line had somehow stayed away from its teeth. There was no sign whatsoever of the original fish.

The shark's mouth was closed tightly over the hook and its eyes bore into Steve's with a predator's malevolence. He looked around him for some useful tool to help, but all he had was a set of tweezers, which were fine for bonefish but slightly under-gunned for lemon sharks. Then his eyes fell on a 2-litre bottle of lemonade on the floor of the boat and an idea jumped into his brain.

Still holding the rod, he picked up the bottle. He leant over the side as far as he dare and tapped the shark on the nose, whereupon it opened its mouth into a snarling gape. Steve immediately rammed the bottle into the shark's mouth, picked up the tweezers and went to work on the treble.

It was actually the shark's furious head shaking that enabled the tweezers to pull the hook free, and there then followed a wild few seconds of mad thrashing around from the front end of the fish while the boatman, to give him his due, held onto the rope manfully at the tail end. The shark was furiously ripping into the plastic bottle and lemonade was spraying everywhere, covering the two men in its sticky sweetness.

'Let go!' Steve shouted, and the boatman obeyed, allowing the fish to spring clear.

However, rather than dive away to safety, it proceeded to swim slowly round the boat, eyeing up the two men while it continued to shake its head and rid itself of the final pieces of plastic. Then, with a great slash of its tail, it dived away out of sight and was gone.

The boatman was grinning inanely, out of sheer relief rather than with humour, Steve suspected. The man reached out his hand.

'Very good, sir. Bloody glad it wasn't great white, though.'

BONES, PERMIT
AND TARPON

Fishing for exotic species in spectacular locations and balmy weather is a must-have experience for the saltwater fly-fisher. And the 'slam' is the ultimate achievement.

Bonefish fight with legendary power and agility, especially as they frequent shallow flats, where the only escape from the angler's rod is a seaward run at unbelievable speed. Tarpon, which inhabit pools around stands of mangrove trees, resemble an outsize silver herring and provide a hefty alternative to bonefish, but for the sheer guile and skill required to catch them, perhaps permit are the greatest prize for the globe-trotting saltwater fly caster. To catch all three species in a week is considered a feat, but in a day, practically unheard of.

Nothing quite prepares you for your first sight of a permit. In the flesh they are beautiful fish, which is peculiar, since they are members of the

163

jack family, most of whom are unrefined bullies. Permit are altogether more genteel, even aristocratic, their poise and elegance increased by a heightened forehead that gives the perception of a permanent frown of superiority. They even have a haughty way of rejecting a fly, as though the angler must be something of an idiot ever to think that a permit could possibly fall for such a pathetic imitation. That is, of course, unless the angler listens closely to their guide and is lightning fast on the strike.

On this occasion, on the island of Los Roques off the Venezuelan coast, Robin was getting the distinct impression that his guide, Jose, was anything but impressed with his client's performance. In his defence, Robin reckoned this had as much to do with the intake of vintage rum the night before as his lack of prowess at permit fishing. He had caught plenty of bonefish before, so he knew what he was supposed to be doing out there on the flats. However, he was presently experiencing a rare lack of fishing confidence, with Jose standing close beside him like an examiner and a group of three permit feeding 20 yards in front. His right hand was shaking with nerves as he cast his crab imitation gingerly at the nearest fish, trying not to get too close in case he scared them all away.

'No, man, cast at his *head*.' Jose's exasperated tone, and the way he carefully enunciated each word, said it all. Robin had already missed a permit 30 minutes earlier and his guide was getting understandably fractious. Permit did not offer themselves terribly frequently; they were a fish of the open sea and only occasionally ventured onto the flats to hunt for crabs. Jose quite obviously considered that fishermen were supposed to nail them when they were offered the opportunity. Against the odds, he had put Robin onto these other fish, and wouldn't be happy if there was a mess-up for a second time.

The closest permit was upended and feeding, so was distracted for the moment. Robin cast with more commitment this time, and landed the crab pattern as lightly as he could, just beside the fish. Immediately the fly landed he tweaked it slightly, copying the defence mechanism of the natural animal to get out of the way of the predator.

The permit immediately looked interested at this morsel of food flying in from above, but was not immediately fooled into taking it. Up came the aristocratic brow, frowning as though it didn't altogether believe in God-given offerings from the heavens like this. It swam round the fly, which had now sunk realistically towards the bottom, and then began to upend on the unexpected prey morsel.

'Hit it, man!' screamed Jose.

Robin reacted much more quickly this time and struck immediately, at which point all hell let loose as the permit set off for its more comfortable environment in the open ocean, tearing line off the reel at a mindboggling rate. Robin couldn't believe that he had actually hooked into a permit at long last and realised that he was laughing out loud with pure adrenalin.

This was where the permit showed its true colours. Gone was any pretence at refinement as it reverted to characteristics of the jack family: pure muscle, fearsome speed and awesome stamina. Robin's fish melted 150 yards of line and backing off the reel in a matter of seconds, making him seriously worried about the adequacy of his 16-pound leader. Every time he tried to apply more pressure or changed the angle of strain, the permit reacted by taking more line.

'Watch it doesn't cut you off on the coral.' Jose's grumpiness had evaporated and he now had his arm around Robin's shoulder to steady him as they tried to follow the fish over a bottom liberally strewn with razor-sharp brain corals in 3 feet of water, making it a bit like wading through spiky treacle.

To keep line off the water, Robin was holding the rod over his head as he stumbled along in the wake of the permit, which was very determinedly heading for the edge of the flats and deep water. He was desperately trying to regain some line, all the while wondering how Jose thought he had a chance of controlling what this fish was doing, now at least 200 yards away. All it had to do was flick its tail in a downward direction towards the coral and it would all be over, with very little Robin could do to stop it.

Miraculously, though, it didn't dive, and 15 minutes later, with Robin and Jose having waded, stumbled and even swum at one point over 300 yards, the fish was finally beaten, swimming in a slow circle around the two men. Jose waited for the right moment, lunged in and grabbed its tail, then came up cradling 25 pounds of struggling permit.

'Good on you, man!' Jose's smile split his face. 'I knew you had it in you!'

At this point John, who had been watching the battle from the beach, waded up to congratulate his friend on his debut permit.

'Great stuff! By the way, you can stop smiling inanely whenever you like.'

They photographed the fish and quickly returned it to the water, where it sped away towards the edge of the flats.

Jose was now in his element. 'Hey, John, there were two more permit back there just now. Get your arse in gear, man, and let's have another.'

The fish were still feeding and John, with several permit under his belt in the past few years, was quickly into one on a shrimp fly. The fight lasted 20 minutes, going much the same way as Robin's, except that Jose's part in proceedings was a bit more impressive this time. Having failed a couple of times to tail the circling fish, he threw dignity to the winds and dived full length on the fish, completely disappearing under water for a couple of seconds before emerging with a mouth-splitting grin and an identical fish to Robin's.

Success then went to their heads. Jose, probably sensing an increasingly large tip, suggested that as it was only mid-morning, the duo should go for a 'slam': permit, tarpon and bonefish in the same day. The bonefish should be easy, so they decided to hunt a tarpon next.

'I know just the place,' said Jose. 'It's where the baby tarpon hang out, man. Don't want to get too ambitious on size.'

Jose nosed the flat-bottomed dory in close to a stand of mangrove trees, and they immediately spied the unmistakeable shape of a tarpon just beneath the surface and under a tangle of branches.

Robin frowned. 'I thought you said *babies,* Jose?'

'It *is* a baby, man, it's only about 30 pounds!'

Robin nodded. 'Okay. Er. . . John, why don't you take the tarpon? I haven't a hope of getting a fly under those trees.'

'Like I have?' John snorted.

Jose grabbed the end of his leader. 'Leave it to me, man. Just jump in and keep close.'

Jose and John went in up to their waists, but the bottom wasn't the same as the hard sand closer to shore. Here it was soft, muddy goo, which made movement slow and ponderous. In fact, Robin had the impression of watching two moonwalkers bouncing slowly up and down towards the mangroves.

Amazingly, despite all this commotion, the tarpon was still peacefully minding its own business as John and Jose waded right up to the edge of the mangroves, just a few feet to one side of the fish. John, with his head poked through a gap in the canopy to see what was going on, watched as Jose, taking the fly and a few feet of line in his hand, pushed further into the branches and, like some cowboy attempting to lasso a steer, twirled the fly around before flicking it in front of the tarpon. One tweak was all it took to get the fly engulfed in a huge mouth and John instinctively set the hook.

The tarpon only had to run further into the trees and the fight would have been over before it began. Instead, it decided to head directly for open water, and the route it chose, the most direct one, went straight between John's legs!

With his rod pointed through the branches and both feet firmly trapped in the gooey mud, John couldn't turn, so Robin watched from the boat's casting platform as the tarpon, having reached open water and the end of the available line, started leaping a couple of yards behind John's back. The sight of an enraged tarpon jumping around like a mad dog on a short leash, while John tried desperately to disentangle himself from fly line and mangroves, was enough for both Robin and Jose to dissolve into fits of laughter. However, all this activity quickly exhausted the tarpon, and John was able to salvage what little was left of his dignity by bringing it to hand, as though this was the way one always landed the species.

'Man, watching you English fishing sure is entertainment!' hooted Jose.

Two down and only the easiest of the trio, a bonefish, to catch. Confidence was high enough for them to enjoy a leisurely lunch, then back to the flats for the afternoon. However, the bonefish weren't coming to the table of this particular slam, not helped by the tide, which had dropped back, making the water on the flats very skinny and the fish almost impossible to approach close enough for a cast.

So the day closed in the bar after dinner, with John tending the line burns on his legs and the two of them rueing the lost chance at the big one. Several rums disappeared, before Robin's eyes lit up.

'What time did you catch your tarpon?'

John shrugged. 'About 11.30, I suppose.'

'And what about yesterday, didn't you catch a bonefish in the afternoon?'

John scratched his head, as though trying to think through the rum haze. 'Yeah, I did. A couple, actually.'

'And how many hours in a day?'

'Twenty-four. . .'

'Exactly! You caught a permit, a tarpon and a boney inside 24 hours, which means inside a day. You did the *slam*!'

'I *did*, didn't I?'

'But don't tell Jose.'

'Why not?'

'He'll expect an even bigger tip!'

IRISH EEL ESCAPOLOGY

When a salmon fisherman decided to go after more modest sport, his ghillie took drastic action to salvage his own reputation.

L ough Currane, in the south west of Ireland, is one of the best and most famous stillwater fisheries for salmon and sea trout, and fishermen have flocked there for decades from all over the world. Germans are some of its greatest supporters, often travelling there in the same groups year after year and employing their regular ghillies to guide them.

To get the most out of Currane you have to go afloat, either fishing flies on the drift or trolling lures. And when there are fresh runs of grilse and sea trout in the lough, fishing can be frenetic and very exciting. Such was the expectation one Monday morning, when Herr Schmidt arrived at the boat jetty to go out for the day with a well-known Lough Currane ghillie who, for the purposes of this tale, we will call Patrick.

'Good morning, Mister Schmidt, a grand day for the fishing now, sir, to be sure.'

'Ja, ja.'

'You alone then, sir?'

'Ja, my boat partner, he is not well and stays in his bed, so we go fishing.'

'Hand me your tackle, Sir. It looks like you've enough there to open your own shop!

'Ja, ja.'

The kit was stowed in the bottom of the boat. Patrick thought it slightly peculiar that Herr Schmidt had brought a large tackle box with him and quite so many rods, and even more so that none of them was made up. Anglers normally came out ready to start fishing immediately, but not Herr Schmidt on this occasion. He didn't even start to tackle up as the fishing boat was cast off. Patrick opened up the outboard engine, while Herr Schmidt sat up in the bow seat facing forwards, a large man with ample centre spread, back ramrod straight and hands firmly fixed on either gunwale. If his Austrian Alpine hat, complete with feather, had suddenly sprouted horns, he would have looked every inch a Viking warlord in command of his pillaging longship as they headed out onto Currane.

They motored for about 20 minutes, with Patrick wanting to get to the top of a drift that had produced fish the previous day. He knew Herr Schmidt of old and there was no way he would want to fish the fly. He would be happiest sitting in the middle seat watching the trolling rod over the side as Patrick manoeuvred the boat over the likely lies around the islands. Physical effort was not Herr Schmidt's forte.

As the boat skirted one of the islands, the bowman turned round and pointed animatedly at its shoreline. It was quite clear that he wanted to land, and it looked so urgent that Patrick assumed he must have been taken short and needed to answer a call of nature. Perhaps he had been stricken with the same lurgy as his friend back at the hotel. Whatever the reason, it looked serious, so Patrick ran the boat up onto the island's stony beach.

Herr Schmidt stood up. 'I fish here today, ja?'

'Er. . . what?'

'I fish here from ze island.'

'But you won't catch salmon or sea trout here, Mister Schmidt, sir, you need to be out in open water for them, to be sure, now.'

'No, I fish here today!'

Patrick stared at him, open mouthed. 'Why?'

'Eels, Patrick, eels. I fish for zem today.'

Patrick couldn't speak for a second. In all his career as a ghillie on Currane, he had never, ever been asked by an angler to fish for eels. This was a personal affront to his occupation, a complete lack of respect for his knowledge and experience. How could he possibly go back ashore tonight and tell his peers that he had been fishing all day for *eels*?

Then he uttered words he thought he would never hear himself speak. 'But be Jesus, sir, you'll need worms if you want to catch eels.'

'I have ze worms, Patrick, in my box. I have all zat I need. Please pass me out all my fishing tackle and I vill get set up.'

In a kind of trance, unable to take in what was going on, Patrick lifted the fishing tackle out of the boat and placed it on the gravel shore. However, of one thing he was absolutely certain. He wasn't hanging around the island all day while Herr ruddy Schmidt sat on his backside waiting for something to impale itself on a worm-infested hook.

'If I was you, sir, I would fish down the bottom end, there now. The water is deeper and probably better for eels.'

'Are you not staying with me a little?'

'I'm paid to go salmon fishing, Mister Schmidt, sir; that's my job. So I will see you at lunchtime.'

With that, he pushed the boat off the beach, jumped in and headed for his first drift of the day, praying that he would catch a salmon.

The morning wore on and not a sniff of either salmon or sea trout on the toby. Just before lunch, he tried a drift down towards the island, casting his favourite Olive Bumble on the bob and a Connemara black on the tail, but all he managed was a swirl from a small brownie, and even that didn't stick. He gave up, beached the boat and resumed his job of looking after Herr Schmidt by lighting the Kelly kettle and unwrapping the lunch basket.

' Any luck?' he asked.

'Jawohl! Vun *excellent* eel, nearly 2 whole kilos!'

'Oh, be Jesus, hurrah,' Patrick mumbled under his breath and busied himself with the tea.

After lunch, he left Herr Schmidt to it again. The man seemed in seventh heaven, sitting on his tackle box, with the knowledge that there would be at least one eel to take home to his wife. That put the strongest possible pressure on Patrick. He could perhaps pass off one stray eel if there was something fresh, silver and with an adipose fin in the bottom of the boat. He felt that his reputation depended on the next couple of hours.

'Please, God, just one salmon or a decent sea trout, *please*!' he said out loud.

He passed one of the other boats with the angler in the stern playing a salmon, but he could not stir any interest with his own offerings, not even the smallest of trout coming to the fly, let alone anything big and silver. Then 5 o'clock arrived and there was nothing left for it but to collect Herr Schmidt and take him ashore. It had been a good career. . .

There wasn't just one now, but two eels squirming in a plastic bag that had once held garden peat. As eels went, Patrick had to admit that they were very good fish. The only thing he had against them was that they were just eels.

'Look, look, luverly eels,' cried Herr Schmidt, 'luverly eating. Mmm!'

A cold shiver travelled through Patrick's body from head to toe.

Once loaded up, Herr Schmidt once again sat in the bows like some great Norse chieftain, the peat bag and content safely stowed under his seat. Patrick manoeuvred the boat slowly away from the island, but the more he increased the throttle and the bows lifted up, the more the peat bag slid astern. Once past the toe of the island, he opened up the outboard full tilt and the bag slid serenely towards him and came to rest against a deck board, quietly tipping over to one side.

He suddenly saw his chance and, while Herr Schmidt looked ashore, firmly clutching the gunwales with both arms outstretched, Patrick reached his hand into the peat bag and out over the side went the first eel.

Herr Schmidt was blissfully unaware of these proceedings and was humming to himself, his gaze firmly fixed out ahead, no doubt thinking of the welcome he would receive from his loved one, who obviously shared his passion for eating eels. So Patrick took this heaven-sent opportunity and, quick as lightning, he flipped the second eel over the gunwale.

Alongside the jetty, his worst fears were manifest as he realised that every other boat had caught something. There were either grilse or sea trout for all but his own boat. He jumped ashore.

'Patrick, ze bag, if you please!' shouted Herr Schmidt, and started gabbling away in German to his wife, who had come to greet him.

'Here you are, Mist. . . Oh dear, there doesn't appear to be anything in it, to be sure.'

'Vot? Zere *must* be, Patrick. Vot has happened to my eels?'

'I really don't know, Mister Schmidt. I tell you what, I'll have a look under the deck boards. There might be something down there.'

A couple of the other ghillies came aboard and helped him, while Herr Schmidt looked on with increased bewilderment as it became obvious that the search would prove fruitless.

'But vere have my eels gone?' Herr Schmidt bleated, utterly bereft at this turn of events. His wife didn't look too impressed either.

Patrick stood up, removed his cap and scratched his head.

'Be Jesus, Mister Schmidt, sir, them eels of yours, I can only think they must have eaten one another!'

THOMAS, TIGER FISH AND THE OLD BULL ELEPHANT

An African canoe trip involves an epic battle with rod and line and a reminder that in the bush, as elsewhere, humans must respect their place in nature.

Tom and Julie Davis felt a deep connection with the Southern African bush, having lived and worked there over many years. They regularly returned for holidays and had even become engaged on a previous expedition to the Chimanimani mountains. So it was that they embarked on another African adventure: a canoe trip down the mighty Zambezi, from Chirundu, downstream of Kariba Dam, across the top of Zimbabwe to the head of Lake Cabora Bassa.

'And of course you won't be doing any fishing, will you?' asked Julie, in a resigned, fishing widow sort of tone.

174

Tom grinned sheepishly. 'Oh, I wouldn't think I'll have time. But since you mentioned it, I'll take a small rod, just in case.'

'Yes, I just bet you will!'

So a short spinning rod, fixed-spool reel, wire traces and large spoons with single hooks were included on the equipment list.

They met their guide, Thomas, at Chirundu. 'What is a hippo?' he asked rhetorically, as he started his ritual safety talk about the river and its wildlife. 'A hippo is 3000 kilos or 6500 pounds of pure muscle, all controlled by a brain the size of a ping-pong ball! It sees a boat as competition to chase off; or more likely with you, to bite in half, because your canoe is just the right colour. But don't worry, a hippo always bites the middle of the boat, and you two will be sitting either end.'

'Thanks, Thomas, that makes us feel much better,' said Tom.

Thomas flashed his teeth in a grin. 'Good, because if you end up in the water, that's when the flat dogs get you!'

'Flat dogs?' inquired Julie.

'Crocodiles!'

They made camp the first night on a low lying, grass-covered is-land, on which was the dead carcass of a big male hippo. Strangely, it didn't smell too high, and Thomas was able to show Tom and Julie the animal's incredible incisors, its main weapon, with razor edges that came together in one of the most destructive bites in the nat-ural world. During the night they were serenaded with the constant grunts of live hippos, sounding for all the word like chainsaws, or even ancient seagull outboard engines. To add to the atmosphere, a leop-ard had come through the camp in the night. Thomas had heard its cough and was able to point out its paw prints in the sand, once it was light.

Tom's first attempt at tiger fishing came on an island at lunchtime, which was to become the main window for his fishing, while the other members of the party snoozed in the shade. He soon discovered that tiger fish, very much like chub back in the UK, prefer structures in the river such as fallen trees and rocks. However, as many had found before him, they are difficult to hook, owing to their bony mouths, and the single hooks on the spoon lures were essential to have any chance at all. Nevertheless, Tom began to catch a few small fish of around 1 pound, and he learnt early on to keep his fingers away from the rows of fearsome teeth as he unhooked them and returned them to the river.

On the third day, as they paddled downstream, they came to a series of islets and shoals, which constricted the water flow. This had led to a logjam of water hyacinths completely covering the surface in green leaves, although they were easy enough to paddle through. Just round the next bend, they saw a single huge bull elephant standing in the river up to its belly, gorging himself on the hyacinths and eyeing up the human intruders with what looked like a particularly unwelcoming and suspicious glare. After resting a while to photograph the magnificent animal, they gave him a wide berth and left him in peace to finish his feast.

Soon afterwards, they reached a steep-sided island that looked a safe camping site, all but impregnable from marauding hippos and crocs. They found somewhere to land and haul the equipment ashore, but then Tom used the excuse of impending darkness to scurry away with his rod and net, leaving Julie to set up camp among the acacia trees and then prepare supper. Not very gallant, he admitted to himself, but the area round the island looked heaven sent for tiger habitat; needs must and all that.

He walked to the tail of the island and found that a substantial tree had fallen over and was lying where the two currents, split by the island, came together. It looked great chub water; and that, as he had learnt, meant tiger fish too. He slid down the bank to a small spit of unstable sand, which lost a little to the river every time he moved his feet. Still, he reckoned he had enough time left for some fishing before the spit eroded completely into the river, so he sent out his first cast with the little 7-foot spinning rod.

As the line came round in front of the tree there was a slight tug, but Tom couldn't decide whether it was a fish or one of the submerged branches. He cast again in the same place and let the line come round, whereupon there was another tentative nibble, then the line went solid. He struck and everything went manic, as the tiger fish, much bigger than anything he had encountered thus far, came out of the water and showed all the splendour of its striped flanks, and even its outlandish teeth. It went straight out towards the middle of the current and turned downstream, so that the drag became intense for the little rod and Tom felt himself losing control fast.

His confidence was sapped even more as he was forced to make a sudden move of his feet and a frightening amount of sand disappeared in one lump. With the fish running more or less where it wanted and Tom's fishing platform disappearing by the minute, thoughts of crocodile fangs came very much to mind and he began to fret, although not enough for the moment to abandon a fish like that. Such is the madness of fishing and the Hemingway tradition that runs through it.

It was then that he remembered his Austrian Alpine Club Training from years back, that if he found himself in unstable snow, use his ice axe, fast! So he picked up the net and drove the handle 4 feet down into the sand, then sat down and wound his legs around it. It worked and he felt relatively safe for the time being.

The fish was now heading upstream and such was the continuing drag from the current that Tom was at first convinced that his line had caught round a branch. Then the fish showed again, thrashing the surface and shaking its head so violently that he actually heard the spoon rattle in its mouth. There was only one way he was ever going to get the upper hand with the fish, which was to try to bully it with what little power the rod possessed.

He was just executing this plan, expecting the line to part, the hook to pull out or his beloved Mitchell fixed-spool reel to collapse, when a deep African voice came from behind.

'Kanjan?'

'Thomas, it's you, thank God! Look, I've got a big. . .'

'Stay there, I have a plan.' He disappeared.

Tom sensed that the fish might be tiring a bit now, which was just as well, because it was obvious that he was hopelessly underpowered. He had it floundering around on the surface, although still out in the current, by the time Thomas reappeared with a rope from the canoe, a large loop tied in one end. He lowered it down and instructed Tom to slip the loop over his head so that it sat across his chest and under his armpits. The other end was secured to a tree, which gave Tom the confidence to bully the tiger across the current, away from the sunken tree and within reach of the net sticking up between his legs.

He wasn't quite sure how it all happened from then on, but he was able to extricate the net, pull the fish over it and get Thomas to haul him, the net and the fish up on to dry, stable land.

'That's a great tiger,' drawled Thomas and helped Tom weigh the fish on a spring balance.

'I know what the net weighs,' said Tom, 'so this fish is exactly 4 kilos, nearly 9 pounds.'

'Great tiger, great eating!' stated Thomas. 'We should cook it immediately.'

'No way I'm killing anything as magnificent as this, Thomas. Sorry!'

He used the rope to get back down to the water and watched as the tiger righted itself, hung around for a while and then slipped back into the murky waters of the Zambezi. But by the look on Thomas's face, catch and release was not a philosophy that came naturally to a Zimbabwean used to catching what he could for his family to eat and stay alive.

Tom went back to camp, where his hopes of a fishing hero's welcome were quickly dashed. Julie was less than enamoured at having had to pitch camp and cook supper, added to which she was in the tent trying desperately to free a jammed film in her camera without losing all the images she had taken that day. He crawled into the tent, whereupon he received an earful, especially as he had dragged sand in on his boots and spread it over Julie's sleeping bag for good measure.

'Tom... Tom!' a low, soft, African voice suddenly called from outside.

Embarrassed at someone overhearing the domestic, Tom crawled backwards out of the tent.

'Sorry, we didn't mean to...'

'Shhhh.....'

Tom, still on his hands and knees, looked up to see Thomas with his .303 rifle held at his hip and pointed skywards. There, looming above them and not more than 5 yards away, was a massive bull elephant, rubbing its hindquarters on a tree stump and staring down at what must to him have been two diminutive humans just waiting to be squashed underfoot. His enormous tusks only just cleared the ground and he was quite the most magnificent, and frightening, sight Tom had ever had up close in the natural world. How on earth the elephant had ever climbed onto the island he had no idea, but he was certain it was the same animal they had seen in the river that afternoon.

The tension was broken slightly when the elephant, still scratching its rump, deftly picked up an acacia pod from the ground and lifted it into his mouth. Five more pods and much more backside rubbing followed, but then the elephant seemed satisfied. He stopped scratching, stared down at Thomas and Tom a moment longer, slowly turned around and lumbered away among the trees, eerily silent despite his enormous bulk and the size of his feet.

'That was lucky,' Tom whispered reverently, as though the elephant was still there. 'He could have trampled us to death and not even noticed it.'

Thomas was quiet for a while, then put down his rifle. 'I think he knew you had given your fish back to the river. That meant he wasn't angry with us.'

PERFORMING PIKE

While pike are legendary as master predators, however tough they may be, they are not a species one would normally expect to return from the dead.

Mark Everard is one of the best anglers for coarse fish you will come across in any part of the world. He is also a PhD and an acknowledged specialist on the life history of British fishes. His great passion is catching large roach but, on the occasion that led to the extraordinary sequence of events described here, he was after pike. They were not particularly huge pike where he was fishing, but he hoped he might have the chance of a 20-pounder if things went his way.

He was just putting his tackle into the car when one of his neighbours approached.

'Do you ever catch pike, Mark?' she asked.

'Funny you should say that: they're today's mission.'

'Do you ever eat them?'

'Not if I can help it.'

'I was reading a recipe for pike in a magazine and I think I'd like to try it. It sounds different. Any chance of bringing one home with you?

'Well, I don't mind killing the smaller ones, but I always put big pike back alive. Leave it with me and I'll see what I can do.'

The session went well from the start. Mark had long given up using live baits for pike and instead offered them a herring with an incision down the belly to let the smell of the guts radiate around to attract predators. From the first cast, small jack pike hit the bait, but it was an hour or so into fishing that he had his first take from a reasonable fish. He followed the time-honoured method of hooking a pike: let it run with the bait until it stops, then give it a few seconds to turn the fish round in its mouth in preparation for swallowing it head first and hit it before it does!

The pike fought well, trying to get in among the reeds from where it was used to ambushing its prey. Mark used side strain to keep it out in the open water, and gradually wore it down until he could net it and bring it onto the bank. It was a fish of around 8 pounds, ideal for eating, as it was big enough at that size for the bone-to-flesh ratio to be in favour of the meat, but not too large to lose its flavour and texture. Remembering his neighbour's request, he rummaged around in his box until he found an old wooden priest that he had rarely used and gave the pike two hard raps over the head. He took out the hooks and left the fish on the bank behind him, then went on fishing.

He continued for another two hours, by which time it was getting very cold. He had caught several more pike, one of them close to 15 pounds, but the 20 had eluded him this time. He decided it was best to give in and pack up, so he took down his rods and put the one pike he had killed into a black bin liner for ease of transport back to the car.

He drove home and went straight round to his neighbour's house with the pike.

'Oh dear,' she said, her face twisted in a horrible grimace, 'it doesn't look very nice, does it? It looks sort of. . . mean and nasty.'

'Well, I suppose it is, especially if you're a roach or bream or something. I think it's evolved more to be an efficient hunter than to look nice to us humans.'

She nodded. 'I suppose so. Look, I hope you're not offended, but I don't really fancy cooking that. I mean, the recipe sounded lovely, but it didn't mention those teeth or the eyes staring back at me. Do you mind if I don't take it?'

'Er. . . I could cut the head off and even fillet it, if you thought that would help?'

'I don't think it would. I've already seen those eyes and that mouth, and I'd be thinking of them when I was eating. I'm really grateful to you for trying, but I think I'll leave it this time.'

Mark went home feeling rather miffed. He didn't really like killing pike and had only done so as a favour to the neighbour. He and his family certainly wouldn't eat it, so the fish had died unnecessarily. Mark's conservation background riled at that. It was okay to kill to eat, but anything else was non-sustainable and to be avoided at all costs.

He took the fish out of the bin liner and inspected it. It was a bit muddy and had some grass on the flanks, so he took it to the kitchen, filled the basin with cold water and began to wash it. He was vaguely surprised that rigor mortis hadn't set in; the fish still felt as though it had just come out of the water. The grass bank had been wet and the weather cloudy and cold, so it had kept moist and there was none of the deterioration in quality that sometimes happens on hotter, sunnier days. However, it was still something of a shock to feel the pike twitch as he washed it, and even more so when it opened its mouth in a sudden snap. Fortunately, his fingers weren't in the way.

Mark inspected the pike's head and there were two distinct marks where he had hit it. However, from his ecological training and knowledge of fish skeletal structure, he knew how hard a pike's skull was. He also knew that pike, like eels and even carp, can survive a long time out of water, provided that their skin doesn't dry out too much. Maybe, just maybe, this fish might have survived its experience.

He collected a keep net from the shed, placed the pike inside and put both carefully into his garden pond, making sure the netting was loose enough to allow maximum movement for the fish if it woke up properly. He then went inside for supper.

Early the following morning, Mark received a telephone call from the BBC. It was the producer of a highly popular series at the time on the natural history of angling, *Tales from the Riverbank*, on which Mark was an adviser.

'We've got a problem, Mark. We're doing a programme on the biology of freshwater fish and we need one of the top predators. Where can we get a pike at short notice? We're filming on the Thames today, but we're hoping to do the tank shots in the studio in the next couple of days; we need something of up to 10 pounds or so and we need it fast!'

'Hang on a minute. . .'

He went out to the pond and, as he gingerly lifted the keep net out of the water, the pike kicked its tail. Mark inspected its head and the mouth and gills were opening and closing quite normally. It had not only survived, but was behaving just how a live pike was supposed to.

'I can be with you in a couple of hours with an 8-pound pike. Any good?'

'How the hell. . .?'

'Don't ask, it's a long story.'

Mark put a couple of buckets of water into two bin liners doubled up, then trapped as much air as he could by quickly grabbing the bag opening together in his fist and winding it down to tie off and make a taught balloon-type structure. In the absence of neat oxygen, this is an ideal way of transporting fish, allowing the oxygen from the air to dissolve gradually into the water. The bag went into an old cardboard box to give it some stability, and they set off for the studio.

The pike performed brilliantly for the cameras and was destined to become the star attraction in 'Pike – Myths and Monsters'. If you see a recording of the episode, this is the pike with the characteristic, well-healed scar on its flank from some far-distant run-in with a bigger pike. Clearly, this was a fish with a charmed life!

When filming had finished, the producer came over to Mark.

'Well, I think we've finished with the pike now. We'd better get her back into the river here. There seems plenty of life left in her.'

Since permission is required to move fish to make sure that diseases are not spread unintentionally between rivers, both Mark and the television company had agreements to return fish to the water where they were caught. So the pike was driven back to the original fishing spot, where Mark looked it over once more to make sure it was okay to release, despite the two dents still visible on its head. He slipped it gently back into the river, where the pike slid serenely out of sight towards the reed-beds.

Eighteen months later, Mark received a phone call from a friend. He had been fishing in that same location, and had caught a 12-pound pike.

'I'm sure it's your fish,' he said. 'There's a definite indentation on top of its skull with a smaller one just behind it, and that scar on its flank kind of looked familiar from the television. It certainly looks to me as though some idiot tried to kill it when it was younger!'

PART SIX

Research and Reminiscences

THINGS AIN'T WHAT THEY USED TO BE

Runs of salmon and sea trout are nowhere near as strong on English rivers today as they were in years gone by. One man has some remarkable stories to support this observation.

John Slader grew up with fishing in his blood. His father, Bill, was an avid sea trout and salmon angler when in his prime, while his grandfather, William Bale, was considered by many of his peers to be the finest trout angler on the River Lyn in Devon, south west England, in the latter part of the nineteenth century. In those days, 100 trout in a day was not uncommon, and C F Wade, in his book *Exmoor Streams* published in 1903, referred to one of the pools, Vellacott's, having *scores of salmon, almost as thick as herrings.*

Bill grew up on the banks of the Lyn and in the 1930s, school was just across the river, which meant that on low water he could cross over by jumping from rock to rock. Often he would see an eel's head poking out from a rock, and it was a quick dash into the house to pick up his bamboo cane and return to tempt it from its lair with a worm or piece of meat. We tend to forget in today's world of commercialism and modern fishing tackle that, back in the 1930s and 1940s, times were hard and Bill recalls a Mr Rowe, who owned a shop in Barnstaple High Street, selling bamboo canes with eyes crudely whipped on for sixpence.

Bill's passion for the river inevitably rubbed off on John and, when he was old enough, they would fish together for salmon, sea trout and trout. In fact, John's earliest memory was standing by his father's side at Lyn Rock and retrieving a number one mepps, which was continually attacked by small trout and parr. By the time he was 9, he had caught his first salmon and was already something of a veteran.

John spent his childhood years in Barnstaple and, as he became more independent, he went into cross-disciplinary mode, as happy catching flounders and small bass on the local Taw estuary as he was fishing for dace and roach in the lower reaches. The Taw is not renowned for its coarse fish but in the 1960s, John spent many hours fishing for dace and roach, the latter sometimes touching the magical 2-pound mark. But come July and August he was usually plagued by sea trout, or peal, as they are known in Devon. Coarse anglers hate game species interfering with their sport, and nothing kills a roach swim more assuredly than a sea trout leaping and splashing around!

Despite the roach fishers' disgust, the large shoals of summer peal attracted plenty of fly anglers onto the bank as dusk fell. Bill recalls instances of individual anglers catching 20 fish in a night, and he personally remembers landing 11 fish in two consecutive evenings, even though he never fished on beyond midnight. How the Taw fishermen today would love that many sea trout running the river.

Back on the Lyn, Bill Slader would take a holiday every year and the family would stay on the banks of the river with John's grandparents. One year, with perfect water conditions, John remembers Bill going out early every morning to Watersmeet Bridge Pool and, for 10 days on the trot, he brought a salmon home by 10 o'clock. Indeed, with the river's small pools and the number of salmon and sea trout in them, it was often a problem trying to avoid foul hooking fish.

However, some of the locals were not quite so concerned about foul hooking, just as long as they pulled something out. Poaching was a serious problem on the Lyn and the bailiffs were continually on the lookout for miscreants, although with the deep wooded ravines, catching them was never easy, especially as the poachers, by their very nature, were a crafty lot.

On one occasion, a poacher named Dave was inadvertently helped by Roy, the proprietor of the Watersmeet Tea Rooms, who, having seen the bailiff lurking about, tipped Dave off. Dave decided to head upstream towards Lower Stag Pool and later returned with a bright silver salmon. As he approached the Tea Rooms, he saw the bailiff and, in a moment of panic, he took the higher path to the right of the property; keen to dispose of any evidence, he lobbed the salmon through the fan light of the outside privy. Unfortunately, Roy happened to be sitting there at the time and ended up with the salmon in his lap. History does not relate who ended up eating the fish, although Bill remembers poached salmon sandwiches on the tearoom menu at about that time!

Two extraordinary things happened to the Slader family during those years. First, John was walking along the river, just above Watersmeet, where to access the pools it was necessary to climb down what the locals called the 'Hangings'. The route looked impassable but, by carefully negotiating the steep slope, it was possible to find a way to some excellent runs and pools that were otherwise unfishable.

On this particular summer's afternoon, John made it to the bottom and clambered over a boulder at the tail of a deep pool with the intention of fishing the neck of the next run, which doglegged into a narrow gully of fast water. As he prepared to cast, he suddenly realised that there was a salmon lying on a slab of rock in front of him. It was still alive and flapping, but had obviously misjudged its attempt to run the falls and was now stranded.

John was faced with the choice of either knocking the fish on the head, as many would have done at that time, or returning it to the river. He had a quick fight with his conscience and clambered down to where the fish was lying. He picked up the salmon, then sat on the rock and held it in the water while it revived. Once he felt the strength return to its flexing body, he let go and it glided sedately away.

He fished on but without success. The following day, he decided to retrace his steps and he fished his way up past Watersmeet until he came to the pool where he had released the fish. His first cast towards the head of the pool with the faithful mepps brought an instant response, and he found himself connected to a salmon that put up a determined fight before he beached it at the tail of the pool. John applied the priest and, as he looked down at the fish, he couldn't help but wonder whether this was the salmon he had saved yesterday. It certainly looked the same size and, even to this day, he has a pang of guilt that he might indeed have killed the very fish he had taken such pains to keep alive. Perhaps it was this experience that made him into the complex being that so many anglers find themselves today: a hunting conservationist.

The other amazing tale happened to Bill. Because the Lyn's pools were so small, fly-fishing was very difficult and the anglers mostly spun or wormed. Bill's favourite spinner was a number five mepps, but they were difficult to get hold of in those days, so he was always especially careful not to lose one if he could possibly help it. He would far rather risk injury by wading between the rocks to unhook a snagged mepps than leave it there to rust.

On this occasion, Bill hooked a salmon, a good fish of about 10 pounds that fought hard and required plenty of rod action to try to control it. At one point Bill was too hard with the side strain and the line broke, allowing the fish to take away his precious mepps. Cursing his luck, Bill sat down to tie on another swivel and spinner and, just as he was finishing, he looked into the water, at the edge of the pool, and saw a salmon rubbing its mouth between two small boulders. In its jaws was the number five mepps!

Bill stood up and set his tailer, which was a common means of landing a fish in those days. He quietly lowered the tailer into the water and with one fast, deft movement, slid the loop over the salmon's tail and held it on a tight rein before lifting it out of the water. Back then, in times of plenty, there was no hesitation in despatching the fish before recovering the precious spinner.

The postscript to this story is not such a happy one. A couple of years ago, John was visiting his elderly parents and, it being August after a period of heavy rain, decided to take a trip down memory lane and pay the Lyn a visit. With the river in flood, conditions looked ideal and, if the river lived up to its reputation, it should be teeming with salmon and sea trout.

He arrived at the river at lunchtime, fully expecting there to be so many anglers that it would be difficult to park the car. The reality was that there was just one other vehicle in the car park; perhaps everyone had caught their allowance of a brace of fish and gone home early. That had certainly happened regularly back in the 1960s and 1970s, so John set up his rod with a certain expectancy and took the steep descent to the river.

It was at Overflow Pool that he met an angler who, with a friend, had travelled up from Cornwall. He told John that he had just caught a grilse but, to his knowledge, no other fish had been caught recently and those anglers present in the morning had given up in despair and gone home. It transpired that the angler had killed the fish, but it was not the fresh, silver, sea-liced salmon John would have expected; rather, it was verging on being stale and had certainly been around for a few weeks.

John fished until dusk, covering 2 miles of water and fishing all the known pools and lies, but saw not so much as a sign of a fish. The whole experience left him feeling rather sad, and he drove home with the thought that perhaps that grilse in the angler's creel had been the very last salmon to run the Lyn.

Hopefully, we are learning our lessons after the dreadful way we have managed our rivers and their fish stocks and, as a result, one day the fish will once again surge through the runs and crowd the pools. Until then the Lyn, and so many other English rivers, remains but a shadow of its former, glorious self.

FROM WHITEHALL TO THE GREAT BARRIER REEF

Neither retirement nor moving to the other side of the world could stop one fanatical fisherman from catching wonderful fish and helping protect their habitat.

When the Labour party came to power in the UK in 1997, Martin Salter took his seat for the first time. A former Reading councillor who entered local politics to overturn an angling ban on a popular stretch of the River Thames in Berkshire, south east England, this fanatical fisherman was always going to be combining business with pleasure. One of his primary aims from the start was to get a better deal for anglers in the decision-making process, and to see them recognised in their rightful place as conservationists of the aquatic environment. In 2002, he became the Parliamentary

Spokesman for Angling and, with colleagues from the fisheries world as advisers, wrote the Labour Party Charter for Angling in 2005. This was ground-breaking stuff in the UK, and Martin became something of a figurehead for the angling fraternity until he stood down from Parliament at the 2010 General Election after 25 years in public life.

Not wanting to hang around 'after his shift', he immediately set out on a year's sabbatical for Australia, where his wife, Natalie, had taken a new job. He decided to become a freelance writer and occasional consultant, concentrating on the huge variety of fishing open to him from his base in Sydney. He and Natalie rented an apartment overlooking the harbour, where the lure of the water, and the fish within it, quickly overpowered his will to stare all day at the computer screen.

There was a dizzying species list to target, including some of the world's biggest marine fish: marlin, swordfish and blue-fin tuna. Of more immediate interest, while he found his Australian feet, were the fish on his doorstep, those he could catch in and just outside Sydney Harbour. With his coarse fishing background, he decided to use tactics he had learnt from years of fishing for roach on his beloved Rivers Thames and Kennet. His target was luderick, or blackfish as they are known around the harbour, which look like a vegetarian cross between a freshwater perch and a European bass. Their favourite food is green weed and before Martin could start fishing, he had to pick this from the rocky shoreline, with waves crashing in from the Tasman Sea to add a little danger to proceedings.

'Fishing's officially the most dangerous sport in Aus,' said Ron, the first of many new Australian fishing friends. 'We lose quite a few fishers each year, mostly swept off the rocks. Watch it out there when you're collecting bait.'

It wasn't so much the waves as the rock oysters that caused the problems. Razor sharp, they cut into unwary human flesh like a scalpel, making weed collection a quest on its own. Once he had the green weed, though, the sport was frenetic on fish between 2 and 4 pounds, all within sight of the Harbour Bridge. With his 'Pommie' float-fishing skills and a natural propensity to catch fish, Martin quickly made a name for himself among the local anglers.

Outside the harbour, but still with the city skyline in sight, an early-morning 'breakfast' session saw Martin fishing a soft rubber surface lure on light spinning tackle next to a huge buoy marking the navigation channel. His first take was savage, even by Australian standards, and the fish didn't bother to run, but dived straight under the boat, bending the rod so much that its tip disappeared into the water as the reel screamed in protest.

'Kingfish,' said his friend and guide, Phil, as he eased his small boat slowly away from the tackle-snapping anchor chains and towards open water. 'Only one fish out here that fights like that and you've got it.'

Martin couldn't believe the sheer power and aggression of the fish. As he continued to fight it vertically, he kept glancing back at the harbour and city buildings, wondering whether there was anywhere back in the UK where he could be encountering a fish like this so close to a major metropolis. He finally boated a magnificent 13-pound kingfish, looking like an outside mackerel, the source of its power obvious in its deeply forked, predator's tail.

Back home at his computer, he decided to irritate his UK friends by sending pictures of the fight, complete with rod tip in the water and him holding the fish before releasing it back to the sea. The captions revolved around 'Kingfish before work within sight of Sydney Harbour Bridge.' Needless to say, the ploy worked and his friends were totally, enviously irritated, with *all right for some* emails flying around all morning.

Next, Martin took Natalie away for a romantic week at a remote rainforest retreat, Bloomfield Lodge. Situated close to the mouth of the Bloomfield River at the southern end of the stunning Weary Bay, Bloomfield Lodge is a four-hour, rough-road drive from the word's marlin fishing capital of Cairns in Queensland, on the north east coast. The sheer beauty and isolation of the region, sandwiched between the two World Heritage sites of the Daintree Rainforest and the Great Barrier Reef, make the place very special. The oceans alongside the coral sea and the reef are frequented by marlin, tuna, wahoo, sailfish and Spanish mackerel. The reefs themselves hold massive populations of the whole red-fish family, including the beautifully marked Red and Spangled Emperors, large-mouthed nannygai, mangrove jacks and giant trevally. Closer inshore, among the basking crocodiles and wheeling ospreys, barramundi, queenfish, fingermark and threadfin salmon live in the estuaries, river mouths and mangroves that line the many waterways draining the rainforest.

Out on the edge of the reef, Martin fished plastic lures on spinning gear and was immediately hit by a big, 22-pound Spanish mackerel, which fought even harder than the Sydney kingfish. They were then surrounded by schools of bonito and tuna driving baitfish up to the surface and providing fantastic sport on the light spinning gear, hitting the lures as though they were the last food items out in the ocean. Later, fishing closer to the bottom, he hooked into something that he just couldn't hold, which finally broke his line.

'Rock cod or coral trout,' said the skipper. 'He's bust you up on the coral down there. It's lethal against monofilament.'

However, the fishing gods saved the best for the last day. The wind was calm and they were able to take a small boat out to an inshore reef, charmingly named 'Robbie's Knob'. While his colleagues caught brightly coloured orange nannygai on bottom baits, Martin fished fast-moving rubber lures just below the surface. He was just beginning to think that he had picked the wrong option when, out of nowhere, the water exploded as a queenfish grabbed the lure and proceeded to thrash its way across the surface in a shower of iridescent silver and blue. He carefully played this most exciting of tropical sportfish, only to see the hook fall out at the last second. A huge queenfish followed the next cast right up to the boat before turning away, but the third fish stuck fast, and the skipper tailed a beautiful 15-pound specimen for the mandatory photos to be sent to green-faced friends at home.

But the real iconic Australian fish, with something of a cult status among its hoards of hunters, is the weird and wonderful barramundi, distant relative of the mighty Nile perch. It is weird because it frequents both salt and fresh water, and all barramundi are born male, only turning female later in life and definitely by the time they reach 17 pounds in weight. The much sought-after yard-long specimens are therefore all females and get very angry when hooked. They are the reverse of Atlantic salmon and sea trout, in that they spawn in the tidal reaches rather than the headwaters of rivers.

Martin travelled to the great floodplains of the Northern Territories, to Arnhemland Barramundi Nature Lodge, in the heart of the country's largest Aboriginal reserve. Perfectly timed to coincide with three days of neap tides, he joined guide Benn Boulton out in the bay where, almost immediately, he took a small barramundi from among the snags of the intertidal zone. Once the tide began to flood, though, Benn took the boat up the tidal reach of the Liverpool river and started to troll over a prominent rock bar.

'I reckon this is one of the best places in the whole country for barramundi,' Benn said. 'This is where we get the big ladies when they shoal up in May.'

Martin was just about to ask 'What about now, in October?' when his rod lunged over and a shell burst from the water, its silver flanks shimmering in the afternoon sunlight. It continued to spend most of its time in the air as it completed a couple of circuits of the boat, and a magnificent 32-inch fish, weighing well over 11 pounds, was netted into the boat. Once photographed, it was returned to the water to become one of the grandmothers of the future.

Over an ice-cold beer in the lodge, Benn reflected on the plight of the barramundi, about its commercial over-fishing in the past and the chemical pollution in some of its most important river and intertidal habitats. The discussion went on long into the night about the need to protect fish stocks and their environments on a global scale, the very issue for which Martin had fought so hard in his UK parliamentary days.

Of course, Martin's angling exploits, carefully written about in articles for both Australian and UK publications, together with his politician's ability of telling people what he felt needed to be done to improve the lot of Australia's fish stocks, its anglers and their regulation, inevitably led to a call back into the political arena. Not to stand for the Australian Parliament, but to author an Aussie version of the Charter for Angling, which had been so successful in putting the issues into the public eye in the UK.

'I think this sort of thing is destined to be my lot in life,' Martin remarked in an email back to the homeland. 'I just can't get away from bloody fishing politics!'

It will be a worthwhile legacy if the Australian state and federal governments take heed of what he says, as the policy makers were beginning to when he left office in London and packed his fishing kit to go global.

UNCONVENTIONAL TACTICS

There are many ways of catching fish. Just occasionally, conventional methods go out of the window in order to bring the quarry to hand.

Ben Juckes fished from an early age, growing up, as he did, in the Gloucestershire countryside in the west of England. He cut his teeth as a young trout fisher on the River Monnow in the Welsh borders, a time from which he has two abiding memories. The first was waiting for a dry fly to drift back over a rising fish, only for a kingfisher to dart down the river and land on the very tip of his rod. It looked down into the water from its vantage point, chirped its high-pitched call, then looked back along the rod at Ben. Realising something wasn't quite right with its chosen perch, the kingfisher took off and sped upstream to find another fishing spot away from human interference. So Ben's love of aquatic wildlife was born. And at about this time he was shown how to tickle trout, which was to have a major bearing on a later episode in this tale.

He was hooked on salmon from his teenage years and dreamt of fishing the great Scottish rivers when he could afford them. However, although the English rivers were struggling with their migratory fish stocks by the time he went to senior school, he knew that there was still a reasonable run of salmon up the Severn each year. Apart from anything else, it supported a commercial fishery in the ancient wicker basket putchers down in the estuary, even if the anglers were no longer as numerous in the upper river as they once had been.

The Severn provided the inspiration for another of his passions, rowing, which his school practised at Tewkesbury. With an important regatta taking place the following day, Ben and fellow students went down to the river to set up the course, including anchoring the stake boats below the weir. With rowing very much on his mind, he wasn't, for once, thinking about fish as he walked back to school, and he spent the rest of the evening preparing himself mentally for the next day's sport, in which he was expected to excel.

After breakfast, he went back down to the river to make sure that everything was still all right and that the boats had not been tampered with or, worse still, vandalised. He rowed out to the first stake boat, where all was well, then moved to the second. Nothing was wrong with the boat and the vandals had stayed mercifully clear, but lying in the bottom, on the deck boards, was a magnificent 10-pound salmon, stone dead but still with enough of a silver sheen to show that it had not been in the river long from the sea. The fish had obviously tried to jump the weir in the night and had either missed and gone straight into the stake boat, or had hit the weir, failed to find enough grip with its tail and fallen back onto the deck boards.

Ben stroked the school eight to victory that afternoon and, a couple of days later, the crew were given a special salmon supper to celebrate. However, with his love of fishing common knowledge among his peers, he wasn't sure that he ever managed to convince them, let alone his teachers, that he hadn't poached the salmon from Tewkesbury weir pool. Such is the suspicion that surrounds the fisher.

Ben didn't have to wait quite as long as he feared to fish a serious salmon river. At university in Newcastle in the north of England, he made friends with one of his peers, Richard, whose father owned fishing on the Helmsdale, one of Scotland's premier fisheries and a place where it was usually considered necessary to allow the previous generation to hang up their rods before gaining an invitation to fish.

It can be cold on the Helmsdale in early season but, unlike many Scottish rivers, there is still a healthy run of spring salmon to hunt. Ben was out early in the morning to try to catch a fish before breakfast during his first week on the river. Richard was lower down and out of earshot as Ben started to fish. He had a reasonable hope of a salmon, because the conditions were getting better all the time, with the river level noticeably dropping and the water clearing fast. He hadn't seen any fish yet, but then you don't always see early-season fish on the Helmsdale.

Nearing the bottom of the pool, he heard a distinct *slap* in the broken water right in the tail, which suggested that a fish was running hard and might have stopped in the quieter water. Ben stayed where he was and had a few more casts, letting the fly arc across the tail. Sure enough, his patience was rewarded as the line slowed and he felt a slight knock, as though a small trout had taken the fly. He lifted the rod, expecting to feel the energetic wriggle of a brownie, but instead there was solid resistance and the satisfying shake of a salmon's head.

Ben backed up the bank and furiously retrieved his free line, then tried to horse the salmon further into the pool and away from the attraction of turning downstream through the fast water, where it would be very difficult to follow a running fish. He knew he had to be tough and make sure he kept it in the confines of the pool, otherwise he was sure to lose it.

Alas, the hook didn't hold for long and just pulled free, almost certainly, the ghillie told him later, because it was a tired fish that only took the big tube fly half-heartedly in the first place. That was often the way with running spring fish that had to battle their way through rough water between pools. They would take the fly if it crossed in front of their noses, but you had to be lucky to keep them on for long.

Slightly chastened by the experience, Ben walked downstream to find Richard sitting forlornly on a rock beside one of the lower pools.

'What's up?'

'I've just lost a bloody fish!' cried Richard. 'I had it right in close to the bank here, almost in the net, and the hook came out.'

'Bad luck. And snap, I've just done exactly the same.'

Richard snorted. 'We're a right pair, then, aren't we? I can't understand where mine went, mind you, because it certainly didn't swim back into the middle. I think there's a hole that's been scoured out near the bank in the winter floods and it's sulking down in that.'

'Whereabouts?'

Richard pointed. 'Down there somewhere.'

The river had dropped even more since they started and Ben could make out a depression at the edge of the pool that looked as though it had undercut the bank. He carefully eased himself into the river, then bent down and steadied himself with one hand on the bank while he felt underneath, as though back in his childhood tickling for trout. He slowly made his way along until his hand brushed against something unmistakably tail-like. He lunged a bit further forward, grabbed the tail wrist and hauled the salmon out into open water.

'Bloody hell!' cried Richard, 'you miracle worker!'

'Misspent youth,' said Ben, modestly, holding the fish in both hands now and supporting it just below the surface. 'What do you want to do with it?'

Richard looked as though he was fighting with his conscience. He could, after all, walk into breakfast clutching a spring salmon and receive the plaudits of the rest of the party. On the other hand . . .

'Hold it there, Ben, while I take a couple of pictures.'

That done, and on Richard's instructions, Ben pointed the fish into the pool and allowed it to swim away into deeper water and safety. They both walked back to the house with perfectly clear consciences, but a great tale to tell over porridge.

Later, at about 4.30 on Saturday afternoon, with the light beginning to fade and the end of a fishless week looming, Ben had another gentle take, the line just stopping in mid-channel where he knew there were no snags. He lifted into the fish and felt the rod jerk with the first head shake, then the salmon fought him all over the pool for the next 10 minutes, for the most part staying deep and feeling doggedly solid. Gradually, though, he was able to work it into the shallows and finally had the fish on its side ready to net.

What Ben did not realise at this point was that he was standing on a similar length of bank to the one from underneath which he had extricated Richard's fish. As he lent forward with the net, the undercut bank gave way and he was propelled head first into the river, into considerably deeper water than when he had been tickling for salmon. He managed to keep hold of his rod but, freezing and shocked, it was a major struggle to get back to the bank lower down the pool and somehow haul himself out with his chest waders full of water. He was soaked through and perishing cold, but he collected himself and wound in the slack line onto his reel, the last thing he was thinking about at that moment being the salmon he had just lost. All he wanted to do was to get back to the house and out of his wet clothes.

Suddenly, the rod arched over and he was amazed to find himself playing the fish again, although it was exhausted by this time so didn't put up much resistance. He brought it to the bank near the bottom of the pool and, net-less now, he waded in and tailed his salmon, which he quickly realised was his biggest ever by some distance. With freezing cold hands, he managed to open up his tape and measure the fish at 35 inches, then he let it swim away to freedom. The table later confirmed a weight of around 18 pounds.

Not a bad way to end another average fishing week, he decided, as the sun set in a wonderful red glow in the western sky and he squelched his way towards lodge and a hot bath.

MAHSEER AND FUNERAL
PYRES

India is a mysterious, magical country, where spirituality lies at the root of everyday life. Fish play their part in that alongside humans, in both life and death.

T he Hindu religion sets a broader context for much of what happens in many Indian communities, especially those in more remote, rural areas. And it is here that India's most prized fishing quarry, the mighty mahseer, is to be found. But when Mark travelled to the border between India and Nepal, little did he suspect how fishing and religion would come together to create one of the most remarkable events in his global angling experience.

It is important to understand the Indian approach to death and the cremation ceremony. The cremation burns a dead body over flowing water, often at the sacred confluence of two rivers, a place known as a sangam, where almost invariably there will be a temple. The cremation returns the departed to the five elements. This starts with the spirit having already left the body, so the ceremony is an act of celebration as much as an activity surrounded by mourning. The flame of the pyre is for cleansing any impurities and returning to fire that which is of fire; the smoke takes the body into the air; and the earth swallows up the ash. Finally, the river takes away what is left, as the burned remains of the pyre are pushed into its current to finish the process.

Mark began fishing for mahseer with his Indian guide, Gagan. He alternated between plugs and fish baits for this voracious predator, backed up by heavy tackle to handle the fish in the fast-flowing water at the confluence of the Saryu and Kali Rivers. The cliffs on either bank create an awesome, densely wooded Himalayan ravine through which the river flows, swelled by the melting glacial water from way back in the upland valleys. It was as awe inspiring a place as it was possible to imagine for a fishing trip, and Mark felt incredibly small within that fantastic landscape.

He had plenty of opportunity to watch the wildlife, because the mahseer weren't playing for the moment. A couple of tentative hits on the plug had failed to connect with fish, and that was all the first morning had to offer. However, disappointment was tempered by the constant spectacle of common, giant and pied kingfishers darting up and down the gorge, pausing to perch on rocks and branches and fish in the quieter water away from the swift, mid-channel current, before moving on to feed their young.

Over lunch, a procession of people carrying branches started to thread its way down the steep valley side, piling the timbers neatly in the shallow margin of the sangam.

'What's going on?' Mark enquired.

'Someone must have died in one of the outlying villages last night,' responded Gagan. 'They're just building a pyre to burn the body over water opposite the temple. Look, there's the dead body now.'

A group of men carried the wasted figure of an old woman on branches, a limp arm flopping out from under the gaudy funeral silks that barely covered her corpse.

'Let's hang back here out of their way and watch,' Gagan suggested. 'You'll be able to see one of our finest local traditions.'

'Er . . . sounds interesting, but what about the mahseer?'

'Come with me to the temple. I think you will find it a very spiritual experience that will also inspire you in your future fishing here.'

The funeral ceremony was unbelievably moving. The dead woman was obviously a grandmother, if not a greatgrandmother, judging by the extended gathering of men around the pyre. The women, by tradition, either kept away from this holy rite or watched half-concealed in the surrounding forest. The dead lady's trailing arm was tenderly returned to her side on the pyre by her son as he lit the fire. But there was nothing ghoulish about it, nor did there seem any feeling of sadness among the mourners. If anything, it was a joyous occasion as they watched the fire progressively consume pyre and body in a mass of flame and smoke.

'This is an incredible experience,' Mark whispered to Gagan after a while, 'but which bit of it is supposed to be inspiring my fishing?'

'It is nearly time. There, look!'

The fire was burnt down by now to glowing cinders, a few charred timbers and goodness knows what else left in the middle of it all. Some of the menfolk now came forward and proceeded to push the smoking remnants from the shallow margin into the swirling currents of the main river. As the smouldering debris hit the water, the most amazing thing happened. The water began to boil as fish of all sizes rolled on the surface, slashing at what was coming down into the water from the funeral pyre.

Mark stared open-mouthed at the scene. 'Bloody hell!' he muttered. 'Are they eating what I think they're eating?'

'Of course! Anything that is left from the pyre is consumed by the fish. All is returned to the air, water and earth, one way or another.'

'And they're all mahseer down there?'

'Not all, but they are mostly mahseer.'

'They're *huge*!'

'Some of them, yes,'

'Hey!' Mark looked around to make sure no one else was listening. 'Pity we can't fish down there now. I mean, that's what you call serious ground baiting, isn't it?'

Gagan put a hand on his shoulder. 'Now, it's extremely interesting you should say that, because there's something I've wanted to do here for a very long time. If you are agreeable, I think that time has arrived.'

'Er . . . you're not thinking of knocking someone off and . . .?'

'No, no, no!' Gagan laughed and clapped him on the back. 'But I have a plan. I think that tomorrow we will give it a try, just down there, away from this sacred site, but still close enough . . .'

The following day, Mark arrived to find Gagan already stacking dried timber from the surrounding forest into a funeral pyre. Mark helped him finish the construction, not daring to ask, or even guess, what they were actually going to cremate.

Gagan was finally happy that they had reproduced a funeral pyre as close to the real thing as they were able. 'Now, you must tackle up with your strongest line. I am expecting the very biggest mahseer to be attracted to the water below, and you must be ready to intercept one of them.'

'What do I use as bait?' asked Mark, not sure whether he actually wanted to know.

'I have your bait ready for you. Tackle up now and I will be back shortly.'

Mark put up a rod and multiplier reel loaded with 40-pound line. He was nervous, not only because of what Gagan was about to do, but also whether or not they would be caught doing it. It was obvious from the surreptitious way in which Gagan was behaving that this might not be well received by the other villagers if they found out, and the last thing Mark wanted was to upset the locals and risk being run out of the area. All the more so as he hadn't yet caught a mahseer.

Gagan reappeared after a short while, dragging something along in a large sack. It was obviously heavy, and Mark's nerves deepened as he watched his guide with growing suspicion. Gagan upended the sack and out fell a very dead sheep.

'Thank God for that!' Mark cried in relief. 'Here, let me give you a hand.'

They plonked the sheep on the pyre, Mark wishing he had had the forethought to tie a bandit-style handkerchief over his nose. Every mahseer in the neighbourhood must be able to smell this animal from miles away, and they would surely be forming a queue down below to eat their fill.

Gagan lit the pyre and the flames began to build round the interlocking timbers. 'It is important that everything is as though this was a genuine cremation,' he said. 'The fish must not suspect anything is different. And now for your bait.'

Gagan produced a large lump of mutton, which Mark impaled on the hook. They then waited for the fire to do its work, until it was time to kick the remnants into the river, just as had happened yesterday.

'Be ready to cast out your bait,' said Gagan, 'right into the middle of the fish. One of them will most definitely take the sheep meat.'

In went the charred timber and what was left of the sheep, the pungent smell of burnt mutton pervading the air. Mark waited, poised for the action to start.

Nothing happened! The wood floated away on the current and the rest of the debris sank out of sight, but not a single fish showed on the surface. Gagan stared into the water. He was speechless and was muttering something under his breath. It seemed to Mark as though he was meditating or deep in prayer. He stayed that way for a couple of minutes, then suddenly came out of his trance.

'This is very enlightening for me,' said Gagan reverently. 'You see, I now understand that the mahseer must know when a true cremation is taking place. They appreciate that they are part of the ceremony; it is not just food for them, otherwise they would have come for the sheep. This proves to me that the mahseer is, indeed, a deeply spiritual fish.'

Mark ended the week with 14 golden mahseer to his rod, the biggest of which went more than 40 pounds, and all the fish were returned alive and unharmed to the sacred river. He always handled his fish with respect, but found himself treating these mahseer with just a little more reverence than anything he had ever caught before. That seemed only right and proper in the circumstances.

IN SEARCH OF A
RECORD SALMON

Will the British record for rod- and line-caught salmon ever be beaten? One angler's in-depth research suggests there is one river that could host such a giant fish.

Many people would say that the day of huge salmon running British rivers to spawn has passed. There was a time when commercial netsmen regularly caught massive fish, and rod and line fishermen landed, and lost, many salmon of more than 40 pounds. Georgina Ballantyne still holds the record for angled salmon, caught one October day in 1922 on the Glendelvine beat of Scotland's River Tay. The story of that fight has passed into legend: she just 18 years old and her father controlling the boat on the oars, before finally gaffing the mighty fish. Hooked in the afternoon, the fish was eventually landed in total darkness and weighed exactly 64 pounds.

Georgina's fish took a minnow lure, which means that Mrs Morison's 61-pounder from the River Deveron is the largest fly-caught salmon. Perhaps there is something in the myth about women catching more, and bigger, salmon than their menfolk after all. But with nothing heavier being caught in the decades that had passed since those monsters were beached, Andrew Graham-Stewart decided to play the fish sleuth and see if there were any signs of a remnant population of leviathan salmon that might one day produce the record-breaker.

Few people have greater access to records than Andrew, and after a great deal of research across the major salmon rivers of Scotland, one emerged as a genuine candidate for an outlandish fish: the Brora, in the north east Scottish Highlands. This modest river system in Sutherland drains just 165 square miles, as opposed to, for instance, 2500 for the Tay catchment, and so its propensity to produce very big fish will surprise many. But as Andrew delved deeper into the statistics and spoke to people who knew the stories, he unearthed some amazing tales of Brora leviathans. True, many of these colossal salmon were caught a long time ago, but the staggering fact was that the river was not known for especially big fish in the 1800s, while perhaps the biggest of the lot appeared in the river in the twenty-first century.

Interestingly, Andrew discovered that eggs had been brought over from Germany's River Rhine, well known for its huge salmon before pollution killed the stock, in the late 1880s and their progeny stocked into the Brora. Although few of these stockings were ever terribly successful, it may be that the Rhine genes are still present in a few fish to this day and so produce the occasional monster.

The list of great Brora salmon started in the 1920s, when Charles Akroyd, one of the great anglers of the era and inventor of the Akroyd strip-winged fly, landed a salmon of over 40 pounds. In the same decade, legendary local ghillie John George Edwards was taking a nap behind a wall while his charge, a woman once again, fished down the famous Bengie pool. He woke up to see that her line was moving steadily upstream, whereupon he sprang to his feet, grabbed his gaff, waded into the water and, at the first opportunity, lunged at the fish as it swam past and dragged out a 45-pounder. No heroic, hours-long battle with this fish, and few such enormous salmon can have been landed quite so quickly.

Then, shortly before the Second World War, a head keeper named Dunn took a fish of 48 pounds from the Madman pool, which remains the biggest salmon ever caught in the river on rod and line – the emphasis being on the word *caught*! A clue as to what was to come happened just after the war, when a local lobster fisherman and well-known poacher, known as Otan, was in the habit of setting an illegal net at the mouth of the river while he hauled his pots out in the bay. On this occasion he found a huge fish entangled in the net, which he managed to keep hidden while he landed his catch and then found a willing buyer in the shape of the local butcher. History relates that this fish weighted 65 pounds, a smidgeon more than Georgina Ballantyne's record.

One autumn in the early 1950s, Jock Wilson, brother of local tackle dealer Rob Wilson, fished the Bengie Pool in drought conditions. As usual in these situations he used a single-handed rod, in this case a 9-footer with floating line and an 8-pound cast. A big fish came to his fly but stopped short of taking, and followed this with six more suspicious looks at successive casts before it finally lost its inhibitions and was hooked. Jock reported that the fish was in control for the vast majority of what ensued, with him hanging on while the salmon swam in continuous circles round the pool.

After about an hour, Jock became fed up with this and waded out as far as he could into the pool, waited for the fish to come past on its prescribed course, and managed to sink his gaff into its flank behind the head, whereupon the gaff handle promptly snapped off. He described what followed as a submarine continuing its unwavering circular route around the pool, periscope raised, and none of the pressure Jock was able to exert with his inadequate tackle had any effect on the fish at all.

Eventually, the salmon began swimming increasingly closer to the bank on each revolution, until Jock was confident that he could actually reach it. He picked his moment, dropped his rod on the bank and threw himself at the fish, managing to get both hands underneath it and then wrestle it from the water and onto the bank. It was a silver cock fish and, remarkably, had taken the fly, had obviously still been suspicious of it and had spat it out through its gills before Jock could strike. The fly had embedded itself in the salmon's shoulder, and it would probably still have been swimming round the pool the following morning had Jock not taken the initiative when he did. It weighed exactly 40 pounds, but one last twist to this tale came when, having been sided and hung up to smoke, it fell from its hooks and was incinerated by the fire.

Jock's fish shows one of the problems of trying to land large fish on smallish rivers. To have a serious chance of beaching, say, a 50-pounder, one really needs the river space for the fish to take off on long runs and so tire itself out. On a river like the Brora, with comparatively small pools, they could spend all day swimming round and round and never get sufficiently tired for the angler to gain enough control to net or beach them. Even so, several anglers came tantalisingly close in the years between 1970 and the early 2000s.

In about 1970, the local police sergeant reported seeing a salmon the size of a pig in the lower river, and Rob Wilson's father saw it in the Bengie later on. The following evening, Rob foul hooked it on a dry fly and, although it didn't stay attached for long, he said it produced the most amazing bow waves that came ashore on both sides of the pool. Later still an upstream tenant, known as Stuffy Steven, hooked it on light tackle and proceeded to be played by the salmon, following it wherever it went and crossing fences some 60 times before eventually, after two hours and with the angler far more exhausted than the fish, the hooks broke free. The postscript to this fish story came in December, with the discovery of a putrefying skeleton on the Blackwater tributary. Scientific analysis of its jawbone suggested an original weight of at least 65 pounds.

In the mid-1970s, a Mr Chevalier hooked a big fish in April in the upper river, but lost it after half an hour. In early June, estate owner Richard Tyser saw a group of black-backed gulls feeding on the riverbank, and found the remains of a huge fish that had died of the devastating disease of that time, ulcerative dermal necrosis or UDN. These remains weighed 38 pounds, so what the whole fish would have been we can only surmise.

The most recent encounter with a really big salmon was in October 2001. Captain Tim Ritson and party were fishing the lower river, three weeks after a 38-pound fish had been caught. Captain Ritson and retired Helmsdale ghillie Donald MacKay fished the Well pool and lost a salmon of around 25 pounds at the net. Soon afterwards another fish took gently and went into a sulk, first on their side of the river, then moving to the far side and refusing to move an inch.

From Donald's experience, he was convinced that the fish was over 50 pounds, as he and the captain took it in turns over the next hour to try to prise the fish away from its lie. Eventually the massive fish moved remorselessly down the pool towards the weir, seemingly oblivious to the pressure from the 16-foot double-handed rod bent over to maximum power. With Donald on the rod, the captain made sure he was in position to see the fish as it slipped over the weir, and suggested that it looked more like a shark than a salmon.

The fish then settled in the rough water at the head of the New pool below and became as immovable as before. However, a while later they saw the fish rubbing its mouth on the gravel bottom, and this eventually broke the nylon.

The following February, a local ghillie, Donald Cameron, found a decomposing female salmon kelt at the tail of the Bengie pool, half a mile or so downstream of the New pool. He and head bailiff, John Bray, showed it to Richard Tyser, then chairman of the Brora Salmon Fishery Board, and they measured it at 54 inches long, the same as Miss Ballantyne's Tay fish. However, although the state of the salmon made it difficult to measure the girth, it was certainly greater than the $28^1/_2$ inches recorded for the Tay fish. Taking a safe bet of 30 inches, and averaging out various accepted formulae, a weight of between 61 and 75 pounds was estimated.

Sadly, by the time Andrew Graham-Stewart heard about the kelt and went searching for it with the idea of mounting the skeleton for posterity, it had been ditched into Loch Brora because of the horrendous smell. However, the evidence is there that leviathan salmon still occasionally run Scotland's rivers. And if you had to put your money on the river to break Georgina Ballantyne's ancient record, then look no further than the Brora.

ROACH TO PERCH TO MONSTER PIKE

Youngsters like nothing better than experimenting with fishing techniques and learning from experience. Reading magazine articles can conjure up dreams of catching a monster; and just occasionally, the dream comes true . . .

I n the 1960s, when boys were still allowed to go off fishing on their own, Greg and Richard were given permission to fish in a beautiful private lake in the grounds of a manor house on the border between Surrey and Sussex in southern England. They had no real idea what fish were in the lake and, at 10 years old, they only had very basic angling skills in any case.

They left their bikes in the lane against the fence running round the property. Full of excitement about this first ever trip on their own, they grabbed their tackle, jumped over the stile and ran across the field to the lake.

It was just as Richard had imagined it would be: a large area of open water, with lily pads dotted around the edges and out towards the middle. There was even a small island close to the shore, so there was a narrow channel running between where they were standing and the island. It looked the ideal place to start fishing.

Their tackle was rudimentary: cheap fibreglass rods that both boys had been given as Christmas presents, small fixed-spool reels and straightforward float, split shot and hook arrangements on the end. Bait was equally simple: white bread, which they wetted down and kneaded into a stodgy dough.

The island channel proved to be a great place to catch small roach. Almost as soon as the float settled itself in the water, it started bobbing up and down and then slid under. The fish were not very big, just a few ounces, but it was great fun and went on for about an hour before they stopped biting.

'I'm going to try spinning,' said Greg. 'I bought a mepps in the tackle shop the other day.'

'Okay, let's see then.'

Greg bit the hook off the line, slid the shot and float off and tied on the mepps. He carefully flipped back the reel's bail arm and flung the spinner towards the centre of the lake. Over the next half an hour, he became quite proficient at lobbing the spinner for up to 40 yards into the lake and winding it back at different speeds, as he had been told to do in a magazine article he had read about spinning.

Richard was sitting on the bank, feeling a bit bored with the lack of action from his float.

'I've got something!' Greg shouted.

Richard looked up to see the rod bent and Greg carefully reeling in a fish splashing across the surface. It wasn't much bigger than the roach they had been catching, but it looked different.

'Hey, it's a perch!' cried Greg.

Once on the bank, they had a real problem extracting the treble hook from the little fish's mouth. When they finally managed it, they quickly threw the perch back into the water but, rather than swimming off, it floated slowly away on the surface. They watched it drift out beyond the island, vainly hoping it would revive, when there was a massive swirl on the surface, momentarily destroying the peace of the lake, and the perch disappeared. The ripples fanned out in an increasing ring, lapping first against the island and then gradually working their way to the bank where the boys were staring, gobsmacked.

'What happened?' Richard asked.

'Something huge ate the perch. Must have been . . .'

'A pike!'

Greg nodded. 'Must have been, mustn't it?'

The two boys couldn't get the vision of that great swirl out of their minds. They talked about it for the rest of the day and agreed that they just had to try to catch that fish.

Having read another article on pike fishing, Richard went into town on the Friday and took his pocket money into the tackle shop while his mother was buying groceries next door. He came out with a wire trace and two treble hooks, and a recommendation from the tackle dealer to buy some sprats from the fishmonger for bait.

Saturday morning saw the boys on the lakeside again. Greg had borrowed his father's sea-fishing rod and big wooden 'Scarborough' reel, loaded with suitably strong line. They tackled up, tied on the wire trace and mounted one of the sprats as the magazine article had showed them: one hook in the head, the other just behind the dorsal fin.

Greg cast the sprat out, although he needed a couple of goes to get it in roughly the right place, just to the left of the tip of the island, where the pike had snatched the perch. He rested the rod in a forked stick and they settled back to see what happened.

Nothing stirred in the first hour and they decided to try some roach fishing again, although their concentration kept switching from floats back to the big reel, which had been left with its ratchet off so that line could easily be pulled off.

'The reel moved!' Richard shouted.

'Are you sure?'

'Yeah, I definitely saw it. *There*, it went again!'

Greg threw down his roach rod and picked up the thick fibreglass sea poker.

'Remember what the man in the shop told me,' said Richard. 'Let it run with the bait until it stops.'

Greg nodded, his eyes glued to the tip of the rod and his hand lightly feeling the reel. Then it began revolving again and this time it kept going as line was pulled steadily off the drum. The anticipation was unbearable.

'Wait . . . *wait!*' Richard encouraged.

The line stopped and Greg braced himself.

Richard put a hand on his arm. 'Just a bit longer. Remember what that article said: he's turning the fish round in his mouth so he can swallow it head first.'

Greg nodded again. His hand was shaking and his face grimaced with tension. 'Now, you reckon?'

'Yeah . . . *now!*'

Greg leant back and put everything into the strike. The rod bent in a great arc and then line shot off the reel as the fish headed out towards the middle.

'Ratchet!' cried Richard.

Greg flipped the brass knob on the side of the reel to engage the ratchet, which made a horrendous rasping, metallic noise as the fish bore away.

'What do I do now?' cried Greg.

'Put your hand underneath the reel to stop it!'

Greg cupped his hand under the revolving drum, gradually increasing pressure until the fish slowed down. He was then able to regain some line, until the fish changed direction and darted to the right, the line cutting through a lily-bed; several large green leaves were severed from their stems and floated free.

Somehow or other Greg managed to hang on to the fish, letting it run away when it wanted but always managing to stop it before it reached the dense lilies in the middle of the lake. Slowly, over the next half hour or so, the runs became less energetic and the reel drum slowly filled up with line, until finally the swivel on the wire trace came out of the water and there was a swirl as the fish surfaced.

'Blimey!' shouted Richard. 'How are we going to land *that?*'

Greg had borrowed his father's net, but there was no way this pike was fitting inside it.

'Dunno. Look round for somewhere we can pull it out.'

There was an inlet to the shore where a boat had been pulled up onto the grass. The bank had been worn down there and was shallower than anywhere else. There was a bush between them and it, but it was the only place they had a chance of beaching the fish.

'Follow me.'

Greg began to walk the fish round. It occasionally tried to run out into the lake again, but it was tired now and couldn't make much headway against the heavy glass sea rod. Richard went round to the other side of the bush and pushed himself as far into it as he could, then reached over and took the rod as Greg sprinted round to join him. At least Richard was able to feel the huge fish on the end for a few moments, although his heart came into his mouth at one point as it violently shook its head in a last-gasp effort to throw the hooks, and he thought he was going to lose it. Then Greg grabbed the rod back and they quickly reached the sloping bank.

'How do I do this?' Greg gasped.

Richard had hatched a plan. 'Don't reel in any more. Just slowly walk backwards and I'll grab it when it gets in the shallow bit.'

'*Don't lose it!*'

The strategy worked and soon the pike was floundering with its back out of the water. Richard caught hold of the trace and held it tightly, while Greg threw down the rod and jumped into the water behind the fish. Together, they rolled it up the bank, well away from the edge.

'I don't believe the size of it!' shouted Greg. 'It's huge!'

'What now?'

'Kill it! I've got to show Mum and Dad, haven't I?'

'Okay.'

There were paddles in the boat. Richard took one and handed it to Greg. 'Go on, it's your fish.'

Greg held the blade end, took careful aim and brought the handle of the paddle crashing down on the pike's head.

'Again, just to make sure.'

He hit it again twice, whereupon a great shudder went through the pike's body and it lay still. They knelt there for ages, gazing down and admiring the fish in disbelief that this was happening to them. Eventually, they collected the rest of their tackle into the knapsacks and looked around for something to help them carry the fish. Greg found a branch that he broke off to a manageable length, which they stuck into the pike's mouth and out through its gills. They took one end each and struggled across the field and over the stile with it. They tied the rods onto their bikes, then rode back to Greg's house very slowly, side by side and still clutching the branch between them.

The epilogue to this story is that the lake owner was delighted the pike had been removed, because she thought it had been responsible for eating all the ducklings in the spring. Greg's father was so delighted with his son's efforts that he paid to have the pike set up in a bow-fronted glass case, and it hangs in Greg's home to this day.

The brass plaque reads: *Pike 21 lbs 8 ozs caught August 1966 by Greg Wright aged 10 years.*

DYNAMITE AND GOONCH

A species of fish in India has an evil reputation but puts up a terrific fight. So could the locals ever learn to love this alleged man-eater?

Nothing has ever been proven, but there have been reports from some parts of India of children being dragged under the water by invisible river monsters. There does happen to be a large catfish, called a goonch, which could be the culprit; certainly many Indians think so. It is tailor-made for villainy: huge bony whiskers, piggy eyes, unattractive dirty brown body and a very wide mouth. It can reach 450 pounds or more in weight, and is definitely open to the accusation of consuming the occasional careless child.

When Mark first visited the border area between India and Nepal, the goonch was public enemy number one in the river. Angling was hardly ever practised along its Himalayan reaches, although nets, snares and other unsavoury methods, such as dynamite blasting and poisoning, were common. Fish of all sorts, even entire ecosystems, were commonly persecuted by people from the surrounding towns and villages, sometimes for food but often just for 'fun'. The fish were literally blown out of the water, although very few goonch were ever eaten. They either died unseen on the river-bed or were thrown away into the forest, with the misguided zeal of those who understood nothing of what they were doing or the ecological impact they were having on the river.

Then an extraordinary transformation happened along the western Ramganga River, because foreigners, the British among them, realised that, despite the dynamite antics of the uninitiated, there were still fish to be caught in the area. Crowning all others was the magnificent golden mahseer, India's fishing jewel and one of the world's hardest-fighting sport fish. So angling people began to visit the area, with its magnificent Himalayan ravine scenery and delightful local people; at least, they were delightful when they weren't blowing up mahseer and goonch.

We know well enough that fishing can add enormously to human well-being. There's even an oft-quoted, and even more frequently pla-giarised, ancient Babylonian saying that time spent indulging in the sport will not count against the fisherman's allotted life span. But it wasn't until Mark's later visit to the Ramganga that he truly appreci-ated the social and economic benefits fishing can bring to remote rural communities, and how angling tourism could change a whole culture within a very short space of time.

Despite the wholesale massacre going on around him, Mark had caught just enough golden mahseer on that first trip to acknowledge the river's fantastic potential, its gorges fed by crystal-clear spring water from the ice and snow melt on the higher Himalayas. However, while waiting during the long periods between mahseer strikes, he regularly heard the dull boom of faraway dynamite explosions.

'What can we do?' his guide, Gaurav, had cried in exasperation. 'How can we ever attract fishermen here while our countrymen act with such barbarism towards our precious wildlife? Think of the damage that is happening right now below the surface with each explosion.'

An aquatic environmental scientist, Mark could appreciate only too well what was happening. 'It's about education,' he had said. 'You've got to make them realise that what they're doing is wrong.'

Gaurav had thrown his hands in the air. 'They will never change. Not while they are hungry and they believe that goonch are taking their children.'

Several years later, Mark was perched on a rock at the bottom of a deep ravine, fishing a bait down a long run of fast-flowing, turquoise-coloured water. Gaurav was again his guide, but gone was the previous depression.

'We can't fit all the people on the river who want to fish here,' he said. 'It's strictly limited by licence now and we are full up throughout the season. The change has been most remarkable.'

'What happened?'

'Just what you said would happen. There is so little money to be earned by the people here, but we have worked with them to take advantage of the large amount of rupees that visiting anglers spend. Instead of bringing supplies for my expeditions, I now phone ahead to ask local traders to stock sufficient to support the needs of my visitors. I have shown some how to run camps and cook for the western palate, and to provide local logistics like ponies and trucks. I have even helped train ghillies and guides for wildlife and cultural tourism. Now these people make a good profit from the visiting anglers I bring to this marvellous place.'

Mark smiled at him. 'The fish are worth more alive than dead?'

'Exactly so!'

'What about the dynamite?'

'Well, of course we can't control it completely. Everyone here has it, as the government supplies it to build mountain roads and clear them after landslides. But enough people now know that by hurting the river they will only hurt their own interests. We have local agreements brokered by some of the headmen in the outlying villages, and also local watchers on the river to stop the killers. No one has heard an explosion here in the past four years.'

At that point, a fish hit the bait hard and line was torn off the multiplier reel. Mark lifted into it and realised this was a powerful fish, but different from anything else he had caught here before. 'Doesn't feel like a mahseer.'

Gaurav was grinning all over his face. 'My friend, I think you have the man-eater himself. If I'm not greatly mistaken, you are fighting a goonch!'

Mark wasn't sure what to think about this. He was after mahseer, but had heard so much about this ugly brute that he was fascinated to see what all the fuss was about. Then the run stopped dead and the line went solid. He pumped the rod as hard as he dare, but couldn't move the fish.

'He's snagged me round a rock!'

'No, no! He's snagged you *between* rocks,' cried Gaurav, laughing now and obviously enjoying himself immensely. 'Now you will see how we really fight the goonch.'

With that, Gaurav picked up a sizeable rock and ran downstream, until he reached a spot roughly opposite where the fish must be lying. He took careful aim and threw the rock into the water. Nothing happened, so he picked up another and tossed that in. On the fourth attempt the fish broke free and ran out more line, but before Mark could react, it all went solid again.

This continued for some while until the fish eventually broke free. Gaurav came back, shaking his head but still grinning.

'You see, the goonch has very strong whiskers either side of its mouth. They are not ordinary barbels; they are supported by bone and powerful muscles. So when the fish is hooked, it looks for crevices in between the rocks where it can anchor itself with its whiskers. Once it is rooted, there is only one way to shift it.'

Mark nodded and continued making up a fresh set of end tackle. He had put golden mahseer to the back of his mind for the time being, because he badly wanted a goonch. He didn't like being defeated by any fish and this was a uniquely serious challenge to his angling prowess. There had to be a way of removing a goonch from a ravine-type river-bed.

He hooked another fish 20 minutes later and a similar fight took place, Gaurav throwing rocks to dislodge the fish and Mark trying clever tactics, none of which worked. Once again, the line finally parted from the constant fraying against rock.

This had become personal between Mark and the goonch. He had fished all over the world and had never given up on a challenge. It was time for a change of tactics, from angling purity to brute force.

It was two hours later that Mark hooked his third goonch. This fish felt heavier, hauling out line against the multiplier's drag as it replicated its colleagues' fighting strategy, finding a suitable niche in the rocks and holding itself fast. This time Gaurav didn't muck around, and he lobbed in a boulder that needed an Olympian effort to propel it over the water. Mark, meanwhile, had moved to a higher position on the rocky bank to change the angle of the line above the fish.

Gaurav's second boulder dislodged the goonch and Mark immediately put his back into the job, frantically pumping the rod to pull the fish away from the rocks. The fight after that was a battle of attrition, the goonch trying to get back to the snags and Mark determined to stop it. Gradually he started to gain the upper hand and after another 10 minutes of blood and thunder, he was able to bring the goonch into the shallows. Gaurav pounced on the fish and held it by the tail.

By the time Mark waded into the water, the goonch had been subdued and he was able to get into position for the photographs. In grand Indian style, he went up to his waist in the river and held the goonch on the surface, one hand supporting it under the throat and the other round its tail.

'It's only a baby,' said Gaurav, looking through the viewfinder of Mark's camera. 'I would say 20 kilos or 44 pounds.'

When the pictures were developed they were classics: Mark with his wild professor's hair and the goonch all piggy eyed, bizarrely whiskered and menacing. But Mark couldn't quite fix the man-eater tag to his ugly protagonist. While it would never displace mahseer as the Indian fisheries jewel, he couldn't help having a sneaking admiration for the misunderstood monster.

ARCTIC SALMON AND ICEBERGS

An iceberg was responsible for the most famous maritime disaster of all time, but you wouldn't normally expect one to play a major role in a salmon-fishing trip, even one inside the Arctic Circle.

The Kola Peninsula, in north west Russia, offers some of the best fishing for Atlantic salmon in the world, but it is an incredibly remote place and can still be freezing cold in the middle of June. It was once a major training ground for Stalin's Arctic troops and has never really lost that sense of military secrecy. This is perpetuated by the entry airport, Murmansk, which has to be one of the most godforsaken places on earth for welcoming tourists: decaying concrete buildings, grass growing through the taxiing apron and numerous wrecked aircraft littering the field.

Added to that, a planeload of anglers can take three hours to clear passport control, so pedantic are the immigration officers, who take an average of at least 10 minutes to process each visitor. Then, before individual groups board the small fleet of ex-army helicopters to ferry them to their respective rivers, everyone's passports are rechecked by border guards looking like clones from a James Bond movie. The only redeeming feature of Saturday mornings at Murmansk airport is the knowledge of what lies ahead in rivers teeming with salmon.

Steve Edge arrived in Russia for the opening week of the Varzuga River season. The trip out to the river was noisy, with nothing other to look at through the helicopter portholes than a flat, snow-covered tundra and the occasional reindeer herd running in panic from the aircraft engines. He had a fleeting vision of being transported out to some Siberian prison camp, never to be heard of again. Then he looked down at the brand new carrying case containing his salmon rods and his heart leapt. He had been dreaming of this trip for months and he couldn't wait to get on the river.

The helicopter landed, discharged the fishing group and its equipment and took off again. For the next six days they were on their own at the riverside camp, out of contact with the rest of the world except via an unreliable satellite phone. Steve usually travelled on holiday with his family, but this time he was alone, although his great friend Nigel was with him and probably still had Steve's wife's warning ringing in his ears, that she held him personally responsible for making sure her husband came home in one piece.

Things started badly. Steve's passion for mixing with people from all countries and backgrounds led him and Nigel to the Russian guides' quarters on the first evening – and a vodka-drinking competition. After several glasses, the head guide, a massive Canadian lumberjack, produced a bottle of near 100% proof liquor, put some into a tumbler and lit it with a match. While the spirit was still flaming, he threw it into his mouth and swallowed the lot in one go.

There came the inevitable question from Steve: 'How hard can that be?'

He took the glass the Canadian offered him, lit it and knocked it back. His eyebrows went first, then the front of his hair caught light and Nigel had to throw a bottle of water over his head to put him out. Somehow the quantity of vodka already consumed made it all seem hilarious, and the competition went on long into the night. No one could remember who won, but the two Englishmen had unearthly hangovers as they prepared for fishing in the morning.

Transport on the Varzuga was by boat and the plan was for Nigel and Steve to motor upstream to their first beat. Steve and his guide were dropped off first, while Nigel and his ghillie went further upstream.

Despite the fact that it was June, the banks of the Varzuga were piled high with ice that had floated down the river on high-melt water flow, only to be stranded as the levels dropped. In places the ice was 7 yards high and gave a surreal Arctic backdrop to a salmon-fishing location. It was also perishingly cold as Steve waded gingerly past the huge boulders and ice blocks along the shoreline, looking for a safe standing in the river from which to launch his attack. He wished the hammering in his head would stop and he made a mental note to lay off the vodka that evening.

The first couple of casts came round without incident, but the third brought a solid take and Steve was into his first Russian salmon. It immediately ran downstream and he began to play it from his position about a quarter of the way across the river, standing in water just above his waist in depth.

Concentrating so hard on the salmon, and with the general background noise of flowing water in his ears, Steve never heard the warning shout from his guide, who had been lighting a fire while his charge started fishing. He just sensed that something was wrong, and he only managed a quick, nervous glance over his shoulder a split second before the block of ice hit him.

Because he was looking round when the ice struck, Steve took much of the force of the impact on the right side of his body, especially in the ribs and a smash in the face. The ice knocked him off his feet and picked him up on its leading edge, so that he was carried down the river as though he were a stranded seal or polar bear. Try as he might, he couldn't fight against the pressure forcing him downstream and anyway, even if he had been able to slide off the ice, its bulk would almost certainly have run him over and crushed him against the riverbed. From the euphoria of playing his first fish of the trip, he was suddenly and bizarrely fighting for his life in an alien environment.

Nigel, motoring up through the rapids above Steve, had seen the iceberg break off from the bank and begin floating down towards his friend's pool. On a hunch, he had ordered his guide to turn the boat round so that they could shoot back and warn Steve. They arrived too late and were confronted by the sight of Steve spread-eagled across the front of the ice flow, being driven unerringly down towards the ocean.

What happened next was a mixture of blind courage and superb boat-handling skills. The guide brought the boat alongside the ice block, picked his moment and, opening up to full throttle, swerved round in front of it, putting them in jeopardy of being run down and smashed to pieces by the berg. As the boat arrived opposite Steve, Nigel leant over the side, caught hold of a wader strap and dragged his friend off the ice into the water. The guide veered the boat off downstream again, ahead of the ice, with Nigel clutching hold of Steve and dragging him with them. Only when they were completely clear did the guide close down the throttle and help Nigel haul Steve over the gunwale and into the well of the boat.

The helicopter wouldn't come back for anything, so it was left to the camp medic to patch Steve up as well as he could, which mainly consisted of keeping him full of painkillers and vodka for the rest of the week. However, probably the best antidote to the agony in his ribs and face was the fact that Steve accounted for 160 salmon to his own rod in one of the most astonishing weeks in the Varzuga's fishing history. Between them the party caught more than 800 fish, several of which weighed more than 30 pounds and a couple over 40.

Steve flew back to London with the rest of the party and reported early on Monday morning to the Accident and Emergency department of St Bartholomew's Hospital. He sat down among a motley collection of drunks, fight victims, children who had various youthful ailments and even a group of scaffolders who had fallen off a collapsing building. It was a far cry from the frozen Russian wilderness, but his ribs and face were still very painful and he had to get something done about them. He settled down for the notoriously long wait endured by patients at major London A&E departments.

Ten minutes later, a nurse came through and looked round the assembled company. 'Steve Edge?' she called out.

Shocked by the speed with which he had risen up the waiting list, Steve followed the nurse, trying desperately to ignore the baleful stares of those who had probably been waiting for hours already. He was whisked in and out of X-ray in no time flat and then, rather than being dumped in a cubicle with a curtain drawn over the front, he was ushered into the senior consultant's office.

'I hear you've been fishing in Russia,' began the consultant, and they went on to talk salmon for the next 10 minutes until the X-ray results came through. 'Right,' he said, looking at the negatives over his light box, 'you've broken five ribs and fractured your right cheekbone. How many fish did you say you caught?'

'About 160. And I would definitely have landed that one I was playing when the ice hit me!'

'The vodka must have been strong to let you continue fishing through that amount of pain.'

'Er, yes, funny you should say that,' muttered Steve, fingering his singed eyebrows. 'Look, doc, I really appreciate you seeing me so quickly. I don't think the rest of your customers were quite so happy about me jumping the queue, though.'

The consultant sat down and grinned across his desk. 'Mr Edge, there was no way I was giving your case to one of my juniors. You see, I have been practising medicine in London for the best part of 40 years and I am retiring in a fortnight.'

'Congratulations, but what's that got to do with my ribs?'

'How else was I going to get on my CV that I'd treated an iceberg victim?'

PART SEVEN

Lost Leviathans

CORNISH MAN-EATER

Many people would be surprised to hear that makos, known man-eaters in other parts of the world, frequent British waters, but they do, among several other shark species. Just occasionally, a mako gets hooked on rod and line. The British record stands at exactly 500 pounds.

The background to this story, which was in Rick's mind as he arranged a week-long sea-fishing trip, would be alarming to most people. A friend of his was a commercial fisherman spending the winter in Cornwall in south west England, hand-lining for the big mackerel that shoaled off the southern Cornish coast in the early 1970s. While fishing among the 300-strong fleet of small mackerel boats a couple of miles off Portscatho Bay, he and his crew witnessed an extraordinary sight: a huge shark jumping inshore, just off the rocks at the head of the bay.

The next day was blowing too hard to go to sea, so they phoned the Fisheries Laboratory in Plymouth to tell them about the shark and ask what it could be.

'Great white,' came the immediate response. 'It probably followed the mackerel shoals across the Atlantic. We've known about them in British waters for years.'

This was before Stephen Spielberg made *Jaws*, so great whites didn't have the global reputation that they do today. Even so, Rick's interest was aroused and he was determined to catch something more interesting than the blue sharks he had hooked many times before on Cornish fishing trips.

Freebooter was based at Dartmouth. She was an old Looe fishing lugger with a distinguished history, including taking part in the evacuation from the Dunkirk beaches in 1940. She was not the ideal angling boat, as her masts and rigging got in the way, but her character made up for that, as did her skipper, Ray Barnett. People joked that his face had more furrows than a ploughed field, moulded from years at sea and an impish sense of fun that meant he was continually laughing. His joking was legendary, although if he ever shouted *let's play sailors* you knew he was being deadly serious.

Rick and his party were on board when *Freebooter* left Dartmouth on this occasion. It was blowing an easterly gale, which meant that the southerly course across to Start Point was very lumpy. From Start, though, the wind was behind them and so the steam down to St Mawes was smoother, with *Freebooter's* mizzen sail up. However, something happened on that voyage that, in retrospect, Rick saw as an ill omen for the entire trip. A particularly heavy gust of wind hit the sail and the sudden pressure snapped the restraining ropes, bringing the boom swinging violently round and smashing into the rigging supporting the mizzen mast. Rick was standing beside Ray, who was on the wheel at the stern of the boat, and the boom missed the top of his head by inches. A foot lower and he would have been killed instantly.

The weather moderated on the Wednesday and Ray steamed *Freebooter* 15 miles offshore, where he turned off the engine and allowed her to drift. The lines were paid out with the baits set at different levels, suspended from balloons that acted as floats. Everyone used mackerel, targeting blue sharks, but Rick had other ideas and had kept some of the pollack he had caught in St Mawes harbour the day before while waiting for the weather to ease. He baited with two fish of about 2 pounds each and let his balloon float a little way further from the boat than the others.

Three small blue sharks came aboard in fairly quick succession and were released, but then everything went quiet for a while. Ray minced up some mackerel as rubby dubby to create an oily slick and attract in the sharks, but they seemed to have disappeared. Even the mackerel became impossible to catch on feathers. It became eerily still out there, as though everything living had disappeared from the sea.

Rick was staring stoically at his balloon when he noticed it dip momentarily under the surface, then it came back and stayed still. Moments later, a sharp fin scythed through the water and circled the float.

'Bloody hell!' cried Ray from the other end of the boat. 'Look at the size of *that*!'

The fin disappeared as the fish dived and Rick picked up his rod. The balloon bobbed a couple of times, then shot under and line began to scream off the big multiplier reel.

Rick let the fish run while he put the rod butt in the fighting pad, then engaged the reel's clutch and struck into the fish. The effect was shattering. The line came cutting up through the water and the sea erupted about 80 metres off the boat. A huge shark came completely out of the water and tail-walked across the surface for several seconds, before crashing back into the sea in a massive plume of spray. More line ripped from the reel as the fish tore off in the general direction of France, and all Rick could do was hang on to the rod for dear life.

'What the hell was it?' someone shouted.

'Bloody great porbeagle,' someone suggested. 'It's a British record if you land that one, Rick.'

Ray shook his head. 'It's too streamlined for a porbeagle. There's only one shark I know behaves like that: mako!'

Someone mumbled something about a fish that size on a cluttered boat like *Freebooter* being an extremely bad idea. Meanwhile, Rick was trying desperately to keep some control over the situation.

Ray came up beside him. 'Let him run as much as he wants. The only chance you've got is to let him knacker himself out completely. You won't beat him any other way with the gear you're using.'

No one actually timed the fight, but the general feeling afterwards was that it went on for more than an hour and a half. The shark made countless long runs, with Ray pouring water on the reel to cool down the effects of friction from the revolving spool against the braking system. Every time Rick regained line the fish would come tantalisingly close, but always staying too deep to show itself. Then, presumably as it saw *Freebooter's* hull each time, it turned and tore off in the opposite direction.

Finally, though, everyone on board saw the big swivel, which joined the monofilament to the wire trace, appear out of the water for the first time, the remains of the burst balloon having slid down the line and clung to it.

Ray ducked into the cockpit and come out with a weapon that was only in there for a joke. He had kept a flying gaff, a huge steel hook attached to a length of 3-inch rope, down there for years, telling different erroneous stories about its uses to anyone who would listen.

Rick eyed up the monstrosity. 'I never thought you were serious about that thing. Will it work?'

'You'd better hope so, because I've got nothing else that'll handle this bastard!'

And then the shark appeared out of the depths, visible from some way down in the clear water.

'Jeeesuuus!' Ray muttered. 'It's even bigger than I thought. We're just not geared up for this size of fish, Rick.'

The shark came up and lay alongside the boat. 'Okay, guys, let's play sailors!' Ray shouted. 'Plan of action: I'm going to try to dig this hook into its tail and get it out of the water. That way it can't run any more. We'll try to tow it in after that, because there's no way that fish is coming aboard my boat!'

Ray went down aft, waited for the right moment and threw the gaff over the shark, then pulled hard on the rope so that the steel stuck fast into the tail wrist. He was just searching for a strong point to tie the rope off when all hell let lose down in the water. The shark's tail crashed against *Freebooter*, so hard that Rick thought it would smash one of the oak planks along the hull. The flying gaff lived up to its name and flew straight back at Ray, hitting him hard on the shoulder before bouncing dangerously around on the deck.

The shark took off and came right out of the water again in another tail-walk. There was a loud metallic noise from Rick's reel, and then the line broke with a resounding *crack*. The shark disappeared.

The flying gaff, that menacing piece of forged steel, had been bent out almost dead straight, as though someone had merely unpicked a paper clip. Ray was clutching his shoulder and the rest of the party were staring from angler to skipper with open mouths. No one spoke for ages.

'Shit, that was the most evil mother I've ever seen,' someone broke the silence. 'Did you see those *eyes* glaring up at us? Evil!'

Ray started laughing nervously. 'Don't worry, guys, he just wanted to eat one of you, that's all.'

Rick stared at him. 'How big?'

Ray shrugged, still nursing his shoulder. 'Say 700 or 800 pounds?'

Rick nodded, a desolate feeling in his guts. 'My thoughts exactly. We never stood a chance, did we?'

Ray shook his head. 'Just stick to blues from now on, Rick, I can handle *them*.'

CAPTURE... ESCAPE...
RECAPTURE...

If the strength of tackle doesn't match the size of fish being played, you need patience and guile to have any chance of landing it. Michael Smith and his team showed both in spades, during surely one of the most remarkable fights with any freshwater fish.

F ew anglers are better qualified to handle a large salmon than Michael Smith. He had already caught a fish of more than 43 pounds, on the Dalguise beat on Scotland's River Tay, so he not only had the experience of landing that fish, but many others of more than 20 pounds and a sprinkling of 30s.

Michael was fishing Scotland's River Beauly in 1986, a system better known for the quantity of its salmon run rather than individual size. However, a few bigger fish were landed each year and the occasional very large salmon had been seen migrating up river in the years preceding this incident. The other relevant issue with the Beauly was that it had a hydroelectric dam at its head, so that the flow could vary significantly over short periods, depending on whether or not the compensation water was running.

The day started with Michael making sure that all the members of his party were settled on their allotted beats. He dropped Bill Hatten off at the island above Breaches pool, then drove down and parked at Minister's. The water was low that morning, with no compensation flow coming through, so he left his double-handed rods in the car and took a 10-foot carbon single hander down to the pool. His reel, a Shakespeare Speedex, was loaded with a full-length slow sink line and about 80 yards of backing. He was using two flies: a shrimp on the bob and a Collie Dog on the point.

He hadn't been fishing long and was working the flies over a ledge that dropped into deeper water when, at about 9.30, he had a vicious take on the Collie Dog. He had a fleeting view of the silver flash as the salmon turned away with the fly and, although he was too far away to guess the size accurately, he sensed that it was much bigger than the norm for the river. His immediate estimate was 30–35 pounds, which was going to be fun on the 10-footer.

The fish wallowed around for a bit, then headed down towards the tail of the pool. Michael followed, wading up to his knees and keeping as much pressure on the fish as he dared, until he reached the ledge and the deep water. The fish was still running and had now taken out all the backing, so Michael was forced to give it maximum side strain to try to turn its head. The rod bent and bent, then bounced back as something gave way.

Michael retrieved what was left, but realised that the whole fly line and about half the backing had gone. There was 70 yards of line out there somewhere, so he ran back to the car and tore up the track to find Bill Hatten. Bill dropped everything and went back to Minister's with Michael, where they climbed into the boat and went searching the deeper water at the tail of the pool.

With the flow so low, the water was gin clear and they soon spotted the fly line lying about 10 feet down. Michael threaded the remaining backing through the rod rings and tied on a treble hook with a small weight, managing to snag the backing with his first attempt. He carefully retrieved it while Bill controlled the boat to make sure there was plenty of slack to play with, so Michael was able to tie the backing braid back onto the reel line and tighten up. To their amazement, the rod arched over and the fish was still there.

The fight was very dogged for the next two hours, with the fish not bothering to run very far but always moving powerfully around the pool. Michael and Bill followed it in the boat for a while, but then went ashore and tried unsuccessfully to coax it into the shallow water. Bill fetched a flask of coffee from the car and, once revitalised with caffeine, they went back in the boat and encouraged the salmon into the deeper water, where Michael held it against the flow in a vain attempt to drown it. The problem was that whenever the fish wanted to do something, its bulk versus the 10-foot rod meant that it was always in charge. There just wasn't enough power in the single hander.

Michael lost count of the number of times the fish went first to the head of the pool, then turned and swam steadily down to the tail. But at about midday, one of its downstream jaunts went a little further and it moved into the glide heading out of the pool. Fearing that the shallower water would spook the fish into a more aggressive run seawards, which would be difficult for the boat to follow with the water so low, Michael jumped out so as to be ready to race along the bank after it. However, the salmon now did a double bluff, turned 180 degrees and bore upstream with just as much energy as it had shown when it was first hooked, leaving a great wake on the surface in its trail.

Michael realised that the line was coming off the reel too quickly for him to get back to the boat in time to follow. He applied side pressure, but it did little good as he watched the last few coils unwind from the spool. At the last moment, afraid that the knot would be blown away, Michael threw the rod into the pool and let the salmon tow it away upstream.

Bill hauled away on the oars and Michael scoured the bottom for the rod, but when they recovered it from among the rocks in the middle of the pool, they found that the backing had broken again, closer to the reel this time.

'Okay, Bill, that's enough. We've given it our best shot and there's no disgrace at losing a fish like that.'

'No way!' Bill cried out. 'We're going line hunting again!'

They searched for another 30 minutes, by which time even Bill was on the verge of calling it a day until Michael suggested they tried one last pass over the original lie where the fish had taken.

'There, it's down there!' shouted Michael. They repeated the retrieval and retying process from earlier and the fish was, incredibly, still attached.

At this point, the fish turned back downstream and then, for the first time, it came out of the water, showing them its true size at last. Its tail slapped back with an almighty splash and there was silence for a second or two.

'Christ, Bill,' Michael muttered at last. 'I knew he was big, but that's just bloody *ridiculous!*'

The fight went on and on, but just when Michael sensed the fish might be tiring, the river suddenly began to rise; the hydro plant had sent down an extra foot of water, so the increased flow turned the advantage completely back to the salmon. It was also harder to row the boat upstream, so Michael took the oars for a spell and gave the rod to Bill.

It was now that the fish, perhaps spurred on by the increased water, changed its pattern and, instead of keeping to the deeper channel and the far side of the pool, headed quickly for a stone croy, stripping line off the reel far more quickly than Michael could row against the flow.

'I'm nearly out of line, Michael!'

Michael had a resigned attitude to the lack of backing by now. 'Okay, throw the rod over the side again!'

Once they had negotiated the croy, they went searching for the rod and managed to gaff it out of the neck of Minister's. The backing had stayed attached this time, so the fight resumed immediately. It was now about 3 o'clock and other members of the party walked down to the pool, bemused at why they hadn't seen their host since first thing that morning. William Wilson, the fishery manager at Loch Leven, had also dropped in on his way back from the Oykel and he offered to take over the oars. A relieved Bill jumped out, and William and one of the party, Hugh, climbed in and resumed the contest, Hugh replenishing Michael's exhausted supply of cigarettes.

The salmon's behaviour now changed, although it still seemed to have as much power as ever. Rather than long runs, it was content to stay close and circle the boat, which gave the three men plenty of opportunity to view its huge bulk. The newcomers couldn't believe their eyes, while Michael was trying hard to ignore the pain in his arm muscles.

Michael finally made the decision to place the boat over the top of the fish and try one last effort to bully it close enough to gaff. This very nearly succeeded on the first two attempts, but Hugh couldn't quite reach it. On the third attempt, with the rod bent as far as it would go and Michael straining everything to get the fish onto the surface, the Collie Dog finally pulled out and they watched, helpless, as the salmon sunk ever so slowly away into the depths of the pool. The time was 5.45 p.m.

The Collie Dog had one of its trebles straightened and another completely crushed. Michael didn't feel particularly upset at losing the fish after more than eight hours, just slightly annoyed that he hadn't fished with the 17-foot double hander, which he was sure would have beaten the fish by lunchtime.

The post mortem that evening couldn't agree on a weight for the salmon. They estimated the length at around 4 feet, but it was the great depth and width across the back that had made it seem so colossal and its true size difficult to gauge. Michael would only say that the fish was definitely heavier than his 43-pounder and would almost certainly have broken the 50 mark, but how much more he couldn't say.

The fish would without doubt have been one of the biggest salmon ever caught in Scotland on a fly, had the Collie Dog stuck a little longer, or the tackle been more equal to the fight, or the hydro plant kept the taps shut off a while longer. As it is, the fish has attained legendary status, and having no idea of the true weight only adds to its mystique.

TEIFI GHOST

The sea trout fisherman is often faced with a dilemma: stay inside and enjoy a glass or two with his companions, or venture into the night in the hope of catching a fish – perhaps a very big fish indeed.

Mike had the yellow hat, the one with the salmon emblem on the front. Its status was a passing nod to the leader's yellow jersey in the Tour de France, although in this case it was worn by the member of the fishing party who had caught the most recent salmon or sea trout. John was irked that he had been forced to hand the hat over to Mike, because the latter's fish had been caught on a prawn and that didn't count in John's book. He had vowed to win it back by fair means, although he was hardly likely to do that with a salmon at the moment. The River Teifi in south west Wales was showing its bones and the salmon were all in the deeper pools and gullies where it was almost impossible to present a fly properly. Only a prawn floated down through the lies stood any chance of luring a fish, but that would be to stoop to Mike's level. So it had to be a sea trout after dark if John was going to wrest back the hat.

'You're just envious because you didn't think of the prawn yourself!' Mike defended his position.

'I wish only to catch fish by cultured means,' John stated with all the fake pomposity he could muster.

'Bullshit!' countered Mike. 'You just forgot to bring your prawn tackle with you.'

John grunted but kept a dignified silence.

'My sentiments exactly,' agreed Robin, the third member of the party. 'If a prawn saves a blank week, bring on the prawn, as far as I'm concerned.'

'Heathens!' muttered John. 'Where are we going for supper?'

After their meal at the Railway Inn, over which they debated the rights and wrongs of fishing with anything other than fly for salmon or sewen, as the Welsh refer to sea trout in their mother tongue, they returned to the isolated cottage and opened a new bottle of malt whisky. Two glasses later and the light was fading fast from the valley. Lights were turned on and the talk turned to sea trout.

'Who's for fishing?' John asked. By the look of the other two, sprawled over armchairs, enthusiasm wasn't great.

'No thanks,' said Mike, looking smug. 'If you remember, I've already caught a fish today.'

John ignored him and looked at Robin.

'I'll go if you go,' said Robin.

'Right, let's get changed then.' A yellow hat was a yellow hat, and he wouldn't win it back by wasting away the precious night hours drinking himself into a stupor.

John arrived downstairs in his fishing kit, but Robin hadn't moved. His enthusiasm seemed to have evaporated along with the contents of his glass. John was faced with two choices: accept defeat and help empty the bottle, or venture out alone to hunt sea trout. He chose the latter, though more from an alpha male, *I'll show you lot* attitude than from any great desire to go down to the river alone. With Mike and Robin's exuberant encouragement ringing in his ears, he crossed the yard and went through the gap in the hedge into the field.

The far-off hoot of a tawny owl greeted his arrival at the Caravan pool and a pair of bats swooped low over his head. It was pitch black now, but John had come to know this piece of water intimately over the years. It was made for sea trout: a deep, ravine-like channel fanning out lower down to form a shallow, streamy tail, which in turn fell away into the neck of the following pool. On the far bank, willows and alders crowded together to form excellent cover for the fish during daylight. This was a perfect sewen pool; always provided, of course, that there were any sewen around to utilise it.

He was standing still, taking in the atmosphere of being beside the river at night, when there came the unmistakable splash of a decent sea trout further down the pool, quickly followed by a second fish. That focused his mind and he started to concentrate. It was no good fishing from up on the bank, so he slid down to the shingle beach from where it was possible to cover the bottom of the pool into the tail. And if sea trout were running, the chances were that they would stop for a rest there, having driven themselves through the riffle between the two pools. Those splashes suggested that was exactly what was happening.

John began to cast across and down the pool, letting the flow work the fly naturally through the main channel, and then figure-of-eighting the line through the slacker water in case a fish was following. On his third cast, there was the definite pull of a sea trout, but it was on and off in an instant. Still, it was all encouraging stuff.

He cast towards the far bank and, as the fly came through the central gully, he had a slow draw of a take, more like a large salmon than a sea trout. He lifted the rod and felt a heavy head shake come through to the butt, then the fish shot into the air and smashed back into the water far more impressively than the two earlier splashes. John's heart jumped a few beats; this was no ordinary sea trout.

The fish took line away steadily downstream and he had to give it some serious side strain to keep it in the pool. The last thing he wanted was to have to follow it through the riffle and into the lower pool, where there were more snags to contend with. The fish then decided that upstream was the way to freedom, and ran back past John at draw-dropping pace before coming out of the water again in two successive jumps. As hairy as this fight was panning out, John's immediate thoughts flew back to the cottage and his whisky-fuelled friends. They were going to be green when they heard about this.

The fish turned and came back downstream and John decided to follow this time, keeping it on a shorter line. He held the rod above his head as he negotiated some chest-high vegetation on the bank, then came back onto the gravel beach just as the fish rolled on the surface near the tail. It wallowed around there for a minute and then, with a sudden surge of energy and despite all the side strain the single-handed rod could produce, the fish bullied itself through the riffle, the splashing of its tail sounding unnaturally loud in the night air as it powered through the shallow water into the pool below.

To follow now meant crossing the river, which John had done before when the river was this low. He waded across the tail and stood in the neck of the lower pool, but when he turned the pressure back on the fish, he felt a solid resistance. There was a moss-covered rock in the middle of the pool that, under normal conditions, was well covered with water, but not at that river height. His heart sank as he realised the fish must have snagged him.

He waded downstream, reeling in as he went until, from the line angle, he knew he must be close to the obstruction. There was little point in keeping light off the water now, so he turned on his head torch and there, ghost-like and perfectly framed in its circular beam just a couple of yards in front of him, was a massive sea trout, lying on its side with its silver flank only barely covered by water. John stared in disbelief at the fish; it must be at least 15 pounds, he told himself, by far the biggest sea trout he had ever hooked. And as he feared, the line was neatly wrapped around the rock, but the fish was practically within his grasp, just a couple of paces forward.

As he took the first step, his foot went into a hidden hole and he staggered forward, momentarily lowering the rod as he desperately tried to steady himself. That released tension on the line, which allowed the fish to drop its head and set off on another run. Backing line raced up the rod rings, round the rock and off upstream, and John wasn't able to follow because he couldn't free the line from the rock without releasing pressure completely, which would have been disastrous. As it was, perhaps he applied too much pressure or the line was weakened at some point. The rod suddenly bounced back and the fish was gone, along with the fly line and a long length of backing.

John stood there for a while feeling stunned, the sight of that fish in the weak torchlight burning ever deeper into his brain. He felt desolate and all the usual self-criticism came into his head: if only he had applied more pressure and kept the sea trout in the original pool, or perhaps crossing the river and changing the angle had been the wrong call. None of it helped, though; the fish was gone and he would probably never hook another like it.

He trudged back to the cottage, which was in total darkness. He poured himself the remainder of the whisky, which wasn't a great deal, he noted, sat down on the sofa and tried to decide how he was going to explain all this to Mike and Robin in the morning. And as he mused, his eyes were fixed firmly on the yellow hat sitting irritatingly on the sideboard.

Ah, well, there was always tomorrow night, and at least he wouldn't have a stinking hangover when he woke up. . .

PALACE PIER MONSTER

Rumours of huge fish beneath a pier were believed by some and discounted by most – but few can have suspected the true size of what was actually down there.

If you read the Introduction to this book, you will know that as an 8 year old I encountered a fish I never saw, but the savagery of the take was such that it haunts me still, five decades later. So even before I spoke to the man in the tackle shop with the hole in the floor, I knew monsters lurked around Brighton's Palace Pier, in among the pilings of the old, rusty landing stage.

I used to let a weight and hook down among the girders to catch the small pouting, bream and pollock that lived down there and were only too eager to grab the piece of lugworm I offered them as bait. I also dreamt that my fish, my mythical bass, would come back one day and give me another chance. It didn't, but I lost plenty of tackle on the ironwork while trying, so I was forever climbing the steps to the tackle shop with the hole in the floor.

246

The hole was about 3 feet square, I suppose, and allowed the tackle dealer to keep a rod lying on the floor, its tip just protruding over the hole and the line disappearing from view. On this particular day he looked pensive when I asked him what he had caught there recently.

'Few bass,' he said, 'and some other stuff. Mainly small.'

'That's not your normal rod,' I said. It had always been an old greenheart, thick as a thumb at the tip and like a tree trunk further down. This was a modern glass-fibre job, though, very out of character with its predecessor.

He nodded. 'Lost t'other one last week. Straight through the trap door it went, gone for ever. Never had no chance of grabbin' it. Must have been huge, whatever it was down there what pulled it in.'

At my age, I didn't even question the story. However, on returning to the landing stage, a group of the regular bass anglers were talking about this supposed incident and laughing their heads off that the old bugger in the tackle shop should ever think he could fob them off with a tale like that.

'Silly sod probably kicked the ruddy rod over the edge when he was stuffing money into the till.'

'What does he reckon pulled it in anyway?' asked another.

'Bloody great whale, I shouldn't wonder,' and they dissolved into another fit of laughter.

All except one. He kept a straight face until his friends had quietened down. 'Actually, I hooked something down here last week that I couldn't move. Never felt anything like it before in my life.'

'Rubbish, of course you didn't. You just hooked the pier again, like you're always doing.'

'It moved,' the straight-faced one said. 'If it was the pier, it was bloody well travelling at the time.'

'Too much beer the night before, if you ask me,' said another, and the laughter went on around the *rap rap rap* on my rod tip that heralded yet another pouting on the end.

I was back several weeks later and the same group of bass anglers were there, fishing into the piles with live pouting for bait. All except the straight-faced one, who had brought along a big-game boat rod, to which he had attached a wire trace, a massive hook and a whole mackerel as bait. I especially remember his mates trying to decide how big the pouting would have to be before it could bite through that wire. They were merciless and, although I found it funny, I couldn't help feeling sorry for the straight-faced one, especially as it transpired that he had been fishing like this ever since my last visit, so convinced was he that there was something outlandish down there among the girders.

I distinctly heard the reel ratchet go. It was not dissimilar to the moment in *Jaws* when the great white takes its first tentative hold of the shark specialist's bait. A few turns of the reel and then it stopped.

'Crab,' said one.

'Bit of weed,' suggested someone else, but I noticed that everyone was staring at the rod, just as I was.

It is difficult to describe the atmosphere on the landing stage, this far detached from the event, but there was a definite feeling at that moment that something out of the ordinary was about to happen. I was gripped by it, watching the tip of the big-game rod with the intensity that only an angler can understand. I was still staring when it was pulled sharply down and the ratchet went again, harder and for longer this time.

'Weed, you reckon?' said the straight-faced one as he grabbed the rod, flipped the reel into gear and struck at whatever it was with all the strength he could muster.

The rod bent, and bent, and continued bending until it couldn't physically bend anymore. Then it stopped, but nothing happened. The enormous power it must be exerting down below wasn't moving anything.

'You're stuck on a bloody girder and the tide's playing tricks on you,' said someone. 'That's no fish.'

Right on cue, the rod started jerking and the line came off the multiplier against the drag as though the Penn Reel company had forgotten to include a braking system in that particular model. The power being exerted was enormous and I wondered, as I'm sure everyone else did, whether the line could possibly stand up to that sort of pressure for long.

I don't remember much about the fight, except that it was a blood-and-thunder tug-of-war, as whatever it was took line, only to be regained by the angler and then about turn as the fish headed back to the bottom with little chance of stopping it. The water was dirty, stirred up by a storm a couple of days before, so we saw nothing for ages except the line cutting through the water. Gradually, though, the man started winning and I suppose 30 or 40 minutes later, with a crowd of anglers, holiday makers, restaurant staff and, of course, the hole-in-the-floor tackle man all looking on, a head came up through the murk.

I can only describe it as though it was a seal breaking surface, the way their heads bob up and down with the rest of their bodies out of sight. This wasn't a seal, but I swear its eyes were fixed on us humans in the same way as a seal stares. In fact, I think the monster was looking directly at the straight-faced angler, and the glare was as menacing as anything I have ever seen from an aquatic beast.

'Bloody *hell*,' cried someone, 'it's a bleedin' great conger!'

'If that bugger comes on this pier,' said another, 'I'm jumpin' off!'

And then I vividly remember the head start to shake and the eel began moving backwards. Its head stayed above the water, but it went horizontally back towards the piles at the other side of the landing stage. Its head moved rhythmically from side to side, presumably in time with its unseen body's squirming, its eyes firmly fixed on the straight-faced one – until the inevitable happened. The wire frayed through and the rod bounced back.

That head – I can still see it now – stayed there for a short time, staring up at us all. Then slowly, ever so slowly, it slid beneath the surface and back down to where its lair must have been, in the ironwork of Brighton's Pier.

The straight-faced angler was desolate, although I doubt his mates teased him very much after that, so there was a silver lining to it all. And they would never have landed the eel, because even the biggest drop net they used on the pier was only designed for a bass or a cod, nothing on the scale of that fish. Years later, when I spent some time in the fishing industry, I handled many conger, some of them very large indeed. I only saw the head of the Brighton beast, but if I had to put a figure on it, I would estimate somewhere around the 60-pound mark. It would certainly have beaten the shore-caught record of the day by a considerable margin.

I left the pier that afternoon feeling rather glad that it hadn't. As much as one likes to see a big fish landed, I was quietly pleased that the conger was still alive under the pier. For the second time in my life,

I had experienced something amazing in the sea and was left with a delicious frustration at not really knowing just how big a glimpsed fish actually was.

I now realise that I had begun to appreciate the mystique surrounding fishing, that inexplicable emotion that goes way beyond the basic enjoyment of merely trying to catch a fish.